Kit & Carolyn Bonner

MODERN WARSHIPS

Evolution

CRESTLINE

First published in 2007 by Crestline, an imprint of MBI Publishing Company LLC, Galtier Plaza, Suite 200, 380 Jackson Street, St. Paul, MN 55101 USA

Crestline titles are also available at discounts in bulk quantity for industrial or sales-promotional use. For details, please contact: Special Sales Manager at MBI Publishing Company, Galtier Plaza, Suite 200, 380 Jackson Street, St. Paul, MN 55101 USA.

For more books on **warships**, join us online at www.zenithpress.com.

ISBN: 978-0-7603-3283-2

Printed in China

On the cover: A long-range photograph taken of a missile being fired by an improved *Ticonderoga*-class cruiser. The USS *Shiloh* (CG-67) as well as a number of *Arleigh Burke*-class destroyers have or will have this system available to defend the United States and its Allies from nations such as North Korea, which has fired ICBMs in the Sea of Japan. At present there are two cruisers near Japan plus several improved patriot antimissile batteries available to dull the threat of North Korea's ICBM program. **Inset:** The USS *Pearl Harbor* (LSD-52) moored at the San Diego Naval Shipyard in 2005. The *Pearl Harbor* is the final ship of the *Whidbey Island* class of dock-landing ships begun in 1985. They are 609 feet in length and displace 15,939 tons full load. Their well deck is cavernous enough to handle two LCACs and the flight deck can accommodate at least two major helicopters or vertical takeoff fixed-wing aircraft. In concert with the big-deck amphibious craft, they are a perfect adjunct to the expeditionary strike group (ESG). *Author's collection*

On the frontispiece: The HMCS Algonquin (DDH-283) makes a speedy exit from Pearl Harbor as she joins other ships from eight nations participating in Rim of the Pacific (RIMPAC) 2006 exercises. This exercise has been carried out for years and hones the skills of the navies that participate. This is another example of coalition warfare. *U.S. Navy*

On the title page: The HSV-X1 (the *Joint Venture* is shown here) is the most revolutionary transport craft yet acquired in the amphibious community. Currently, the U.S. military leases four of these high-speed wave-piercing craft from Australian companies. Along with *Joint Venture,* the *Swift, Spearhead,* and *Westpac Express* have been in constant use since becoming part of the amphibious picture, and a decision has been reached to outright purchase eight craft by 2011.

On the back cover: As of late 2006, the most modern and capable large-deck amphibious carrier: the USS *Makin Island* (LHD-8). This final *Wasp*-class LHD replaced the USS *Belleau Wood* (LHA-3), which was used as a target during a 2006 sinking exercise. The *Belleau Wood* had displayed some deficiencies that were too costly to repair. The *Makin Island* is 844 feet in length; displaces 41,335 tons full load, and has a beam of 118 feet on the flight deck. This LHD carries up to forty-five CH-46 helos (including six AV-8B Harrier II fixed-wing jets) and/or other aircraft such as the Osprey. *U.S. Navy*

Contents

Introduction

Introduction

The end of World War II marked the end of the era of great sea battles but the beginning of one of the most important periods in world naval history. Against the backdrop of potential nuclear holocaust, the Cold War brought technological changes that could hardly have been imagined at the time of the Japanese surrender in 1945.

The post–Cold War era has been one of decline in superpower dominance. At the same time, small nations have built technologically powerful navies, and the role of warships in naval combat continues to change dramatically. Modern maritime technology now can equalize navies. Smaller countries in the littoral regions now have credible naval forces with capabilities once thought impossible but now well within their budgets. For instance, Thailand now has a small aircraft carrier, HTMS *Chakri Narubet*, a well-built command-and-control ship capable of antisubmarine warfare, antiair warfare, search and rescue, humanitarian assistance, and amphibious assault with 675 embarked troops. Surrounding countries have taken notice.

Even the once well-guarded and cherished U.S. Navy's *Aegis* system can now be found on Japanese destroyers, Spanish frigates, Norway's newest frigates, and soon on Korean and Australian destroyer-type warships. And in the free market environment on virtually any and all weapons, Spain, Germany, and Great Britain have all courted Australia with attractive offers to build modern destroyers.

Previous page: The USS *Missouri* moored in Pearl Harbor as a battleship memorial. It is tied up on the famous "battleship row" just yards from the Arizona Memorial off Ford Island. Between the two ships, they are known as the "bookends" of World War II. The USS *Arizona* exploded from a bomb hit in its forward powder magazine within minutes of the December 7, 1941, Japanese attack on Pearl Harbor, and the surrender document between the Allies and Japan was signed on the deck of the *Missouri* on September 2, 1945. *Author's collection*

Five nuclear-powered carriers are moored at the Norfolk Navy Shipyard, including the USS *Enterprise* (CVN-65), the oldest nuclear carrier in the world. Aside from one-half of the American nuclear carrier inventory, the famous shipyard plays host to the command ship USS *Mount Whitney* (LCC-20) and amphibious big-deck assault ships USS *Wasp* (LHD-1) and USS *Saipan* (LHA-2). There are two *Oliver Hazard Perry*–class frigates, a *Ticonderoga*-class cruiser, and two *Arleigh Burke* destroyers as well. The value of these ships represents the most expensive assets U.S. taxpayers own. *Author's collection*

First-generation stealth-type frigates such as the French *La Fayette* class are available to those who have sufficient funds such as Taiwan, which has six vessels that were ordered with heavier armament; the Republic of Singapore Navy, which has also acquired six; and Saudi Arabia, which has opted for three of the very capable ships.

The U.S. Navy is still the most powerful in the world and will be so for the foreseeable future. Soon, it will no longer employ fossil fuel aircraft carriers, and rely upon its nuclear giants. One of the nuclear carriers will take up residence in Japan as the forward deployed carrier since the diplomatic hurdles have been surmounted.

The world's first nuclear carrier, the USS *Enterprise* (CVN-65) will be retired in 2014 when the initial carrier of the CVN-21 class enters service as USS *Gerald R. Ford* (CVN-78). Nuclear carriers are all slated for a fifty-year lifespan due to a number of reasons, including the huge upfront cost to the taxpayers. When the first of the CVN-21 class is commissioned, the U.S. Navy will then have twelve big-deck nuclear carriers.

In the early twenty-first century, a total of nine nations operate aircraft carriers, and all but the United States have selected the small, multitask ships that carry vertical takeoff and landing (V/STOL) or short

An artist's rendition of the improved *Wasp*-class amphibious warfare helicopter carrier. This will be a heavily armed and well-protected amphibious assault vessel that can deliver and support eighteen hundred troops and twice the air group of the current *Wasp* class. This assault ship will be capable of twenty-four knots on gas turbine power, and also can assist immediately in humanitarian missions. It is almost a junior aircraft carrier, and may serve as the model for U.S. Navy carriers of the mid-twenty-first century. *U.S. Navy*

takeoff and vertical landing (STOVL) aircraft, helicopters, and unmanned aerial vehicles (UAVs). The emphasis is not power projection, but multiuse of power for military and humane purposes.

Network centric warfare has been reduced to a terrorist with a cell phone, and war at sea has changed dramatically as well. The specter of a supercarrier steaming through the sea is awe inspiring, like the battleship of the early and mid-twentieth century. Yet, naval warfare has continued to

change as purse strings have tightened worldwide. Nations have been compelled to be innovative in the type of ships they will require in the near term and future. More is expected from today's warships and there are fewer available.

Even the nuclear submarine has proven to be vulnerable to modern antisubmarine (ASW) sensors and weapons, and the quiet-running diesel or fuel cell–electric submarine can elude the best ASW team. In a series of yearlong experiments, the Swedish

The French command ship *Mistral* (L 9013) was built in two sections. The aft section was built in Brest and the forward area in St. Nazaire. After each section was completed, Brest was selected for the launching port. There the two halves were assembled, and one ship emerged. It is a helicopter assault carrier that displaces 21,300 tons full load, and is 199 meters in length. Its air group consists of sixteen helicopters; troop capacity is 450 with 900 during an emergency. *Author's collection*

The *Ticonderoga*-class *Aegis*/missile cruiser USS *Chancellorsville* (CG-62) takes it green as it plows into the sea. This cruiser is one of the twenty-two cruisers remaining in the U.S. Navy because it has the Mark 41 VLS missile launch system and other advantages over the first five ships built in the class. The twenty-two remaining cruisers will be further modernized with new technology and electronics in the near future. *U.S. Navy*

conventional submarine *Gotland* has successfully defeated every attempt that the U.S. Navy's best contemporary antisubmarine warfare weapons and tactics have made to locate and simulate destruction.

The amphibious forces in most navies now predominate in many roles ranging from troop transport and assault to humanitarian assistance. With the big-deck amphibious carriers, noncatapult fighter aircraft are carried as well as a dozen well-armed helicopters. These ships have truly become a multitask platform, and as evidenced by the U.S. Navy's *Wasp* class, and the improved

Wasp class (LHA −R) of four ships promises even more capability. France has already built the command ship *Mistral* (L 9013), and the Spanish Navy's *Strategic Projection Landing Logistics* ship is on the drawing board. All can take advantage of the Joint Strike Fighter and other fixed-wing jet aircraft.

The battleship is no longer part of any navy, and lasted a mere one hundred years (from 1906 to 2006). The cruiser also has undergone a metamorphosis from the mid-twentieth-century eighteen-thousand-ton heavy version and ten-thousand-ton light cruiser to the twenty-two remaining *Aegis*-class 10,142-ton *Ticonderoga* ships in the American Navy.

The F-100 frigate *Alvaro de Bazan* moored in Barcelona, Spain, at a district naval headquarters. The F-100 series is equipped with *Aegis* and a forty-eight-cell Mark 41 VLS missile launcher. This 5,800-ton full-load frigate is considered to be an air defense ship and would serve as an escort for the Spanish carrier or amphibious ships. *Author's collection*

The frigate *Surcouf* (F-711), shown in the photograph, is one of the many *La Fayette* (F-710) frigates that are dubbed stealth ships. They are armed with Exocet antiship missiles, Croatale surface-to-air missiles, and a variety of close-in weapons. The *La Fayette* class has twin propellers and a maximum speed of twenty-five knots. *U.S. Navy*

There are fewer naval shipyards available (eighteen worldwide), and older warships are no longer placed in mothballs on a mass basis. When a navy is finished with a ship, it will be scrapped, used as a target, or become a museum vessel. Most of the older vessels cannot accommodate new technology and electronics.

Navies are quickly moving toward fleets that are composed of inexpensive multifunctional warships. The typical fleet elements the international naval community features today and in the future include the following:

Small multitask carriers that do not rely on catapult-launched aircraft and have an air group of JointStrike Fighters, and helicopters (attack and troop carrying). They must be economical to operate and be capable of virtually any task.

The Swedish *Gotland*-class submarine in dry-dock in San Diego, California. This twin-diesel-powered submarine has two Stirling AIP generator sets and can remain submerged for very long periods. The 1,494-ton submerged boat entered service in September 1999, and has been on loan to the U.S. Navy for a year. It is very quiet running and eluded all attempts by the navy to locate it in test exercises. *Author's collection*

HMBS *Bahamas* (P-60) at its mooring in Nassau. This 375-ton full-load patrol boat can make up to twenty-four knots and was built in the United States. It is armed with one 25mm Bushmaster low-angle rapid-fire gun and has 7.62mm machine guns. Its tasks range from antipirate patrols to arresting smugglers and drug runners in the Caribbean. *Author's collection*

Destroyer-type ships (destroyer, frigate, corvette) that are well armed with cutting-edge electronics and weapons and the ability to add more-advanced equipment.

Amphibious assault ships that can be of the big-deck variety or dock-landing ships with air- and sea-launched craft. These ships must be able to render humanitarian

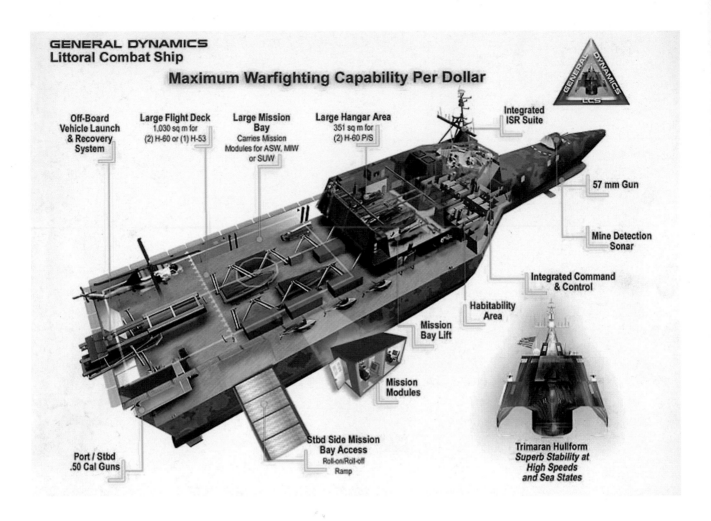

GENERAL DYNAMICS
Littoral Combat Ship

Maximum Warfighting Capability Per Dollar

Off-Board Vehicle Launch & Recovery System

Large Flight Deck
1,030 sq m for (2) H-60 or (1) H-53

Large Mission Bay
Carries Mission Modules for ASW, MIW or SUW

Large Hangar Area
351 sq m for (2) H-60 P/S

Integrated ISR Suite

57 mm Gun

Mine Detection Sonar

Integrated Command & Control

Habitability Area

Mission Bay Lift

Mission Modules

Stbd Side Mission Bay Access
Roll-on/Roll-off Ramp

Port / Stbd .50 Cal Guns

Trimaran Hullform
Superb Stability at High Speeds and Sea States

The General Dynamics version of a littoral combat ship (LCS) will be christened the USS *Independence*. It is capable of virtually all tasks given to the U.S. Navy, and utilizes a trimaran hull for excellent sea keeping and high speeds. This ship as well as the competitor, the USS *Freedom*, takes advantage of new technology and forward thinking in all aspects of LCS design. *U.S. Navy*

assistance, make an assault on an unfriendly beachhead, or complete any number of assignments.

Littoral combat ships that can patrol, do battle with any threat, provide rapid response, and demonstrate a presence in coastal waters.

Submarines that are inexpensive and can elude even the best in ASW-capable warships and aircraft. Launching cruise or guided missiles as well as being special operation capable are also desirable.

Patrol Craft that are multimission capable and able to work in conjunction with the fleet or singularly.

Ships capable of sea-basing for any purpose where equipment, supplies, troops, and military assistance is required quickly.

The capital ship of the future will ultimately be the destroyer, which has crept from 1,100 tons in 1920 to almost ten thousand tons displacement in the early twenty-first century. The aircraft carrier is again much

The American Military Sealift Command hospital ship USNS *Mercy* (T-AH-19) lies off Indonesia after assisting victims of the December 2004 tsunami. The tsunami killed an estimated 300,000 people, and the *Mercy* was on station for five months and treated more than 100,000 patients. This and other disasters have graphically pointed to the need for navies to provide humanitarian assistance as a routine task, and not as an adjunct to their normal duties. *U.S. Navy*

smaller in most navies because there does not appear to be a great need for the supercarriers. More navies will eventually possess one or more of the V/STOL or STOVL aircraft carriers due to the value received and the much lower cost to build and operate.

The littoral combat ship will take center stage because combat and conflict resolution will often take place in coastal areas, and ships able to rescue people who are in eminent danger from natural or manmade catastrophes are and will be at a premium.

Modern Warships provides a perspective of the changes that have occurred since World War II and in particular since the demise of the Soviet Union. In essence, this period has been one where small nations could now have technologically powerful navies, and superpower dominance has declined. Naval combat has moved to the littoral, and the role of warships has changed dramatically. Many of the images that follow are shown for the first time, and provide a unique vantage point on today's naval and maritime affairs.

Post–World War II

Post–World War II

On May 8, 1911, naval aviation became a permanent program in the U.S. Navy, and those who survived eventually joined together to design and wear symbolic wings of gold. At the time, it was a tossup as to whether planes or pilots were most valuable. Every string, wood, and canvas contraption was rebuilt dozens of times after crashes. The other powerful navies were moving at a greater pace, and what was needed were more pilots, aircraft, and an aircraft carrier with dedicated funding.

The American aircraft carrier was essentially follow-on to the British Royal Navy example and their experiences in World War I. Any definition of warships of the early twenty-first century must begin with the marriage of aircraft and warship, and the nation that has built the greatest number and most technologically advanced aircraft carriers in the world. This is the U.S. Navy, which began with a naval aviation laboratory in the form of the coal ship turned aircraft carrier USS *Langley* (CV-1). Six decades and scores of conflicts later, the U.S. Navy now has a number of nuclear-powered 100,000-ton-plus supercarriers and their battle groups continuously roam the seas protecting American and Allied interests.

After the *Langley* entered fleet service on March 20, 1922, those officers who believed in naval aviation knew the upcoming value of the aircraft carrier, but most were young and too junior to make their opinions known in the right circles. By the end of the 1920s, however, the advent of the USS *Lexington* (CV-2) and USS *Saratoga* (CV-3) would change everyone's thinking about the supposed superiority of battleships over carriers in naval combat.

The nuclear carrier USS *George Washington* (CVN-73) leads a carrier strike force or battle group. This group is composed of a supercarrier, *Ticonderoga*-class *Aegis* cruiser, *Arleigh Burke*–class *Aegis* destroyer, and *Oliver Hazard Perry*–class frigate and is backed by a stores (fuel, food, etc.) ship. *U.S. Navy*

The USS *Jupiter* (AC-6), a World War I collier (coal carrier) for the fleet. After the Great War, the *Jupiter* was rebuilt as the aircraft carrier USS *Langley* (CV-1)—complete with pigeon loft to back up the wireless, and cameras to record every landing and takeoff. *Author's collection*

During the early months of World War II, Allied fleets were without any real carrier strength to take the war to the Japanese until the advent of the mass-produced 40,600-ton full-load *Essex*- and slightly different *Ticonderoga*-class carriers. Soon thereafter, the U.S. Navy and its carriers pushed the enemy back to its homeland, and by September 1945, the war came to a conclusion due in large part to the powerful *Essex*- and *Ticonderoga*-class carriers that could hit hard in one area and quickly steam to another to hit again.

After World War II, the three-ship *Midway*-class aircraft carrier was built and

commissioned. There was the USS *Midway* (CVB-41), USS *Franklin D. Roosevelt* (CVB-42*)*, and USS *Coral Sea* (CVB-43). Until this point, the big carrier was defined as an *Essex* or *Ticonderoga* class, but the *Midway*s ultimately displaced more than 64,000 tons full load and were 979 feet in length. They also employed a steel-armored flight deck instead of the wooden decks on the *Essex/Ticonderoga* classes—the damage done by Japanese kamikazes taught the U.S. Navy that an armored flight deck would make the difference between survival and sinking in the future. The size of these

The main U.S. Navy carrier strength in the early 1930s: from top to bottom are the USS *Saratoga* (CV-3), with the black stripe on the massive funnel, USS *Lexington* (CV-2), and the purpose-built USS *Ranger* (CV-4). The *Ranger* was an overall disappointment to the Naval Aviation community, and only served in the backwaters of World War II. *Author's collection*

ships was impressive, and bigger seemed to be better.

As the Korean War came to a conclusion in 1953 when the North Korean armed forces were driven back across the 38th parallel, the United States had deployed eleven of its twenty-five modern World War II carriers off Korea. The jet had come of age, and it was clearly the aircraft carrier that had become an instrument of national and international policy. From the Korean War onward, U.S. presidents continually asked, "Where is the nearest aircraft carrier?" This need of carrier-borne aircraft at the right place at the right time was far more important than the nearest bomber. A decade later, the Vietnam War, included supercarriers with thousands of sorties more than nine thousand days on station. The value of the carrier and supercarrier has since proven invaluable in keeping the United States out of peril. However, today's naval forces aren't as dependent on huge aircraft carriers, battleships, and cruisers. In future naval warfare, big and expensive ships may not be the most effective.

The hero of the June 1942 Battle of Midway—the Douglas Dauntless dive-bomber (SBD). Here a Dauntless is being told to launch when its rpm's are sufficient to get the aircraft off the deck of this *Essex*-class carrier. *Author's collection*

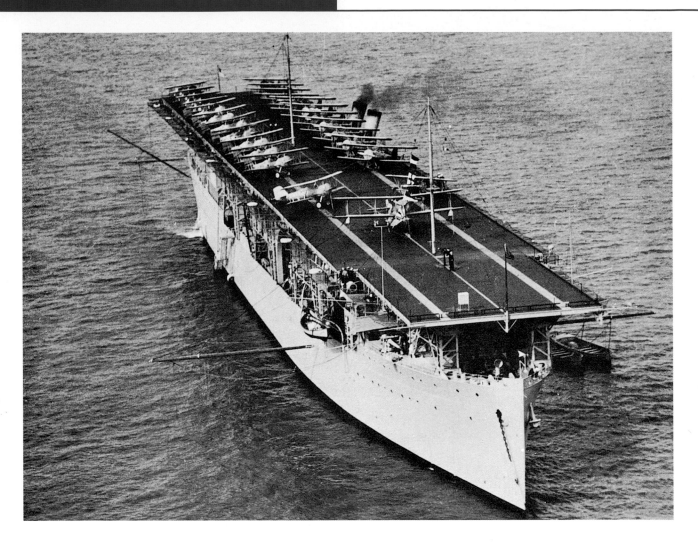

USS *LANGLEY*
Built by the Mare Island Navy Yard
Commissioned: April 7, 1912
Granted to the Naval Aviation Department of the U.S. Navy
    after World War I for aviation experimentation
Allotment to rebuild as an aircraft carrier: $500,000
Recommissioned: March 20, 1922, at the Norfolk Navy Yard
Full-load displacement: 14,700 tons
Length: 542 feet; Beam: 66 feet
Turbo-electric drive: 5,000 shaft horsepower; single shaft
Top speed: 15 knots
Armament: four 5-inch/.51-caliber single-purpose weapons
    and elderly 3-inch guns for antiaircraft defense; few small
    .30-caliber and .50-caliber guns sited around the deck
Aircraft capacity: 33 aircraft of varying types
Crew: 410

The USS *Langley* (CV-1/AV-3) was the U.S. Navy's first aircraft carrier, converted in 1920 from the collier USS *Jupiter* (AC-3), the first electrically propelled ship of the U.S. Navy. In 1937, the *Langley* was cut down to a seaplane tender and became AV-3. After being transferred to the Asiatic Fleet based in Manila, the *Langley* was sunk by Japanese aircraft on February 26, 1942, shortly after the Pacific War began.

A group of pilots in the USS *Lexington* (CV-16)'s air group listen to advice from Lt. Cmdr. Paul Buie. It is vital for pilots to learn from those who have survived air combat. *U.S. Navy*

Ulithi Atoll in the South Pacific. This became the "Murderer's Row" of the big carriers refueling, allowing recreation at Mog Mog for their crews and taking on stores. *Author's collection*

USS *Saratoga* (CV-3, shown) and its sister, USS *Lexington* (CV-2), were the first major carriers built as the result of the Washington Naval Arms Limitation Treaty. Both were former forty-thousand-ton battle cruisers that were converted to aircraft carriers. The *Saratoga* fought in World War II and was sunk during Operation Crossroads during the two A-bomb tests in Bikini Atoll. The ship sank on July 24, 1946.

USS *SARATOGA*
Built by Fore River in Quincy, Massachusetts
Commissioned: November 16, 1927
Full-load displacement: 48,550 tons
Length: 880 feet; Beam: 130 feet
Steam turbines: 209,000 shaft horsepower
Top speed: 33.25 knots
Armament: eight 8-inch/.55-caliber guns/twelve 5-inch/.25-caliber guns. Later, ninety-six 40mm weapons were added.
Aircraft capacity: 90 to 120 aircraft of various types
Crew: 2,791

In June 1950, the Soviet Union tested the resolve of the United States and the United Nations in Korea. The crudely equipped People's Army swept across the 38th parallel and attacked Korean (ROK), U.S., and UN forces near the border. By early July 1950, aircraft carriers of the *Essex* class were launching strikes on North Korean troop movements and supply lines. The USS *Yorktown* (CV-10) prepares a barrier to trap an F9F Cougar with engine trouble. *U.S. Navy*

A Skyraider has just been waved aboard an *Essex*-class carrier operating off North Korea in September 1950. These aircraft carried more ordnance than a World War II B-17 Flying Fortress, and until the A-6 Intruder was introduced to the fleet, they were the bomber of choice for carrier pilots. *Author's collection*

The USS *Oriskany* (CV-34) was the most advanced and modern of the *Essex* class and capable of carrying an atomic bomb–delivering AJ-1 Savage. This made the navy a competitor with the U.S. Air Force for strategic delivery of nuclear weapons. *U.S. Navy*

Later in the USS *Yorktown's* career, the *Essex*-class carrier had been converted to an antisubmarine carrier or CVS. *Author's collection*

An early jet fighter F2H-2 Banshee on the deck-edge elevator on the USS *Lake Champlain* (CV-39) off Korea. *U.S. Navy*

An interesting but grainy photo of an F2H, a McDonnell Banshee coming in to land on the USS *Oriskany* (CV-34) operating in the Sea of Japan. This photo was taken in February 1955 from the gun camera of the aircraft following the Banshee. Landing on a frozen and pitching deck was difficult in the extremis. *U.S. Navy*

The date is February 10, 1955, in the Puget Sound. The former *Essex*-class carrier USS *Shangri-la* (CVS-38) has been given the full treatment and is now a CVS (it was designated as a light-attack carrier until the early 1960s when she became an LPH-8, or helicopter-assault carrier). The *Shangri-la*, along with many other carriers, was refitted to new standards to accommodate larger and more powerful jet aircraft at the Bremerton Naval Shipyard. Later, several of the *Essex* classes were re-created into the first helicopter-attack carriers. *U.S. Navy*

The USS *Yorktown* (CVS-10) rescued the astronauts from *Apollo 8* as well as the capsule that had circled the moon. Astronauts Borman, Anders, and Lovell were in space from December 21 until December 27, 1968. It was the job of stationed carrier groups with SEALs to bring the astronauts and module the final distance. *U.S. Navy*

USS *Enterprise* (CV-6) was the most decorated warship in the U.S. Navy. It earned twenty-one battle stars during the Pacific War, was decommissioned, February 17, 1947, and was scrapped in 1958.

USS *ENTERPRISE*
Built by Newport News Shipyard and Dry-dock, Newport News, Virginia
Commissioned: May 12, 1938
Full-load displacement: 25,500 tons
Length: 827 feet; Beam: 114 feet
Geared turbines—oil fired; 150,000 shaft horsepower; three shafts
Top speed: 33 knots
Armament: eight 5-inch/.38-caliber open mounts, multiple 1.1-inch/40mm/20mm/.50-caliber close-in weapons
Aircraft capacity: 81 to 90 aircraft of varying capability
Crew: 2,919
Damaged often during Pacific War; earned 21 battle stars
Decommissioned: February 17, 1947; scrapped in 1958

Carriers provided much of the air support and air bombardment to the ground forces in Vietnam. A-4C Skyhawks, like these aboard the USS *Bon Homme Richard* (CV-31), carried out some of the first air strikes by the United States during the conflict. By late in the war, the North Vietnamese were well armed with Soviet- and Chinese-made antiaircraft guns and missiles (SAMs). The port city of Haiphong and the North's capital, Hanoi, were the most heavily defended areas in the world against air attack. American naval and air force losses were devastating. Despite speed, electronic warfare, chaff, and heat signature flares, one or more SAMs often penetrated from a large swarm attack, and the wardroom was again missing pilots. It was a difficult form of combat, and only the best "went up north." *U.S. Navy*

The first of the "super" carriers, the USS *Forrestal* (CVA-59) steams at high speed during its trials off the Virginia Coast. Of particular interest is the number of radar-directed enclosed five-inch/.54-caliber guns. This gun battery plus the carrier's combat air patrol (CAP) were the primary means of defending the *Forrestal* against enemy bombers or surface threats. The navy was pleased with the *Forrestal*, yet recognized that improvements were necessary in future ships. *U.S. Navy*

USS *Lexington* (CV-16, shown) was one of twenty-five carriers in the *Essex* Class, the U.S. Navy's premier World War II–built aircraft carrier classes. All of the former *Essex* class have been scrapped or have become ship museums around the United States. Most were retired from active service by the mid 1970s. The USS *Lexington* (AVT-16) became a training ship based at Pensacola, Florida, for a number of years.

ESSEX CLASS
U.S. Navy's premier World War II–built aircraft carrier classes; 25 built
Carriers built by a variety of shipyards to strict plans
Full-load displacement: 36,500 tons
Length as built: *Essex* class, 876.8 feet (short hull); *Ticonderoga* class, 885 feet (long hulled variant of the *Essex* class); long hull built to add two quad 40mm guns forward
Length after modifications (1950s): 894 feet; Beam: 191 feet Steam turbines
Top speed: 33 knots
Armament: changed as war progressed and modifications postwar. Twelve 5-inch/.38-caliber guns, 1.1-inch/40mm/20mm
Aircraft capacity: 80 to 100 aircraft of varying capability from the F4F Wildcat to the A-4 Skyhawk
Note: During World War II, the *Essex* class carried a mix of F6F Hellcat fighter planes/TBF-TBM torpedo-bomber aircraft/SBD Dauntless dive bombers.

A fortunate pilot ejects from his Skyhawk after its brakes failed during recovery (July 2, 1970). The aircraft went over the side, but Lt. j.g. William Belden ejected and made it safely back to the USS *Shangri-la*. U.S. Navy

The forty-thousand-ton full-load USS *Bon Homme Richard* (CV-31) makes smoke and speed off a launching station near the Vietnamese coast in the late 1960s. It was indeed fortunate that the U.S. Navy had several of these medium-sized aircraft carriers to deliver ordnance-to-shore targets and provide ground support for U.S. marines, soldiers, and UN armed forces. *U.S. Navy*

USS *Midway* (CVB-41), USS *Franklin D. Roosevelt* (CVB-42), and USS *Coral Sea* (CVB-43, shown) were built and completed after the conclusion of World War II. They fought in Vietnam and during the Cold War. The *Midway* is a popular museum ship in San Diego, California, while the *Coral Sea* and *Franklin D. Roosevelt* have been scrapped.

MIDWAY CLASS
Built by Newport News Shipyard and Dry-dock Company and the New York Navy Yard
Commissioned: September 10, 1945; *Franklin D. Roosevelt* commissioned October 27, 1945; *Coral Sea* commissioned October 1, 1947
Full-load displacement: 60,000 tons (1945); 64,100 tons (1970)
Length: 969 feet; Beam: 136 feet; 1970 after modifications:
Length: 997 feet; Beam: 258 feet
Geared turbines (fossil fuel): 212,000 shaft horsepower
Top speed: 33 knots
Armament: eighteen 5-inch/.54-caliber guns; eighty-four 40mm and twenty-eight 20mm; later all removed except for CIWS
Aircraft capacity: 80 to 145 aircraft of varying types
Crew: 4,104

Fifty years of U.S. Naval Aviation (1911–1961) are represented by three major aircraft carriers. From top to bottom are an *Essex*-class carrier that has been modified with a hurricane bow andangled deck, the *Forrestal*-class USS *Saratoga* (CV-60), and the *Independence* (CV-62). *U.S. Navy*

The USS *Saratoga* (CV-3) looks small from the open cockpit of a Martin T4M-1 torpedo attack aircraft that was a mainstay of the *Saratoga*'s air group in 1931–1932. The T4M-1 had a top speed of ninety-five knots and a range just more than five hundred miles. It carried a .30-caliber machine gun and a single torpedo. *U.S. Navy*

The USS *Forrestal* (CV-59) was the first of the supercarriers and was one of a four-ship class, which included the USS *Ranger* (CV-61, shown). The *Forrestal* has been decommissioned and will be used as an artificial reef or target. The *Ranger* will be put up for donation as a museum or used as a target.

FORRESTAL CLASS
Built by Newport News Shipyard and
Dry-dock Company, Newport News,
Virginia
Commissioned: October 1, 1955
Full-load displacement: 78,000 tons, which
increased over the years
Length: 1,039 to 1,046 feet; Beam: 252 to
260 feet, dependent on ship
Geared turbines (fossil fuel): 260,000 to
280,000 shaft horsepower, dependent
on ship
Top speed: 33 knots
Armament: eight 5-inch/.54-caliber and later
modern CIWS and BPDMS
Aircraft capacity: 80 to 95 aircraft dependent
on type needed
Crew: 5,265

Later in the life of the USS *Oriskany* (CV-34). The aircraft are larger and more potent. A rescue helicopter is airborne off the carrier's starboard bow, and electronics have replaced armaments. The *Oriskany* was finally sunk to become an artificial reef off the Florida coast in 2006. *Author's collection*

Two Vought O2U-2s begin their landing procedure on the "Sara" circa 1930. These two-seater bombers came aboard in 1928 to form one of the new carrier's first squadrons. *U.S. Navy*

USS *Kitty Hawk* (CV-63) is the lead ship of its class. The others were the USS *America* (CV-66) and USS *Constellation* (CV-64). The *Kitty Hawk* is now the oldest ship in the U.S. Navy barring the frigate *Constitution*. It is forward deployed to Japan until 2008 and will be replaced by the USS *George H. W. Bush* (CVN-77). The *America* has been sunk in experimental work, and the *Constellation* is laid up in Bremerton, Washington.

USS *KITTY HAWK*
Built by New York Shipbuilding Co., New York, New York
Commissioned: April 29, 1961
Full-load displacement: 80,800 tons
Length: 1,047 to 1,072 feet, dependent on ship; Beam: 294 feet
Steam turbine (fossil fuel): 260,000 to 280,000 shaft horsepower, dependent on ship
Top speed: 33 knots
Armament: NATO BPDMS and CIWS
Aircraft capacity: 85 aircraft fixed/rotary wing
Crew: 5,630

The former USS *Midway* (CV-41) makes its way to its final berth in San Diego as a museum ship just after the turn of the century. The ship has become wildly popular in this "navy town." *Author's collection*

The USS *America* (CVA-66), a unit of the *Kitty Hawk/America* subclass of fossil fuel supercarriers has just come alongside a replenishment ship to take on fuel, frozen goods, spare parts, and movies. This 1967 photo was taken by the destroyer USS *Wallace L. Lind* (DD-703). *U.S. Navy*

The USS *John F. Kennedy* (CV-67) was to have been a nuclear aircraft carrier, but at the last moment, Congress was convinced that the cost of the plant would be too high for that fiscal period. They in turn swept the funnel to starboard to at least give pilots a better view of the flight deck. Other carriers that were oil fired obstructed pilot landing with funnel smoke, and the corrosion destroyed many delicate instruments. This was the last fossil fuel carrier built in the twentieth century.

USS *JOHN F. KENNEDY*
Built by Newport News Shipyard and Dry-dock Company in Newport News, Virginia
Commissioned: September 7, 1968
Full-load displacement: 87,000 tons
Length: 1,048 feet; Beam: 252 feet
Geared turbine (fossil fuel): 280,000 shaft horsepower
Top speed: 35 knots
Armament: BPDMS
Aircraft capacity: 80 to 105
Crew: 5,595

Two fossil fuel supercarriers of the *Kitty Hawk/America* class steam together for the last time. Both carriers flew raids against Iraqi military targets day and night during the initial round of Operation Iraqi Freedom. The USS *Constellation* (CV-64) in the foreground is bound for North Island, California. Its battle cry of "Let's roll" is in memory of the heroic passengers aboard ill-fated United Airlines Flight 93. The *Constellation* will be inactivated and decommissioned. Next stop, reserve fleet in Puget Sound, Washington. The USS *Kitty Hawk* (CV-63), now the oldest carrier in the U.S. Navy, will return to Yokosuka, Japan, as America's only forward-deployed supercarrier. In 2008, the aging forty-seven-year-old carrier will be inactivated and replaced by the USS *George Washington* (CVN-73). *U.S. Navy*

The USS *America* (CVA-66) served the nation from January 23, 1965, until used for experiments and sunk off the Virginia Capes on May 14, 2005. The decommissioned carrier is seen in the Philadelphia Navy Yard in November 1999, and six years later was tested over a twenty-five-day period to determine survivability against subsurface and surface attacks. This was necessary to gather data for the next generation of carriers: CVN-21 or CVN-78. *Author's collection*

A storm is about to hit the carrier strike group led by the USS *John F. Kennedy* (CV-67). Consequently, its aircraft on deck are tied down. The aircraft include A-6 Intruders, EA-6 Prowlers, and S-3 Vikings. Soon the Intruders and Vikings will be retired as will the *Kennedy*. With the passing of the *Kitty Hawk* and the *Kennedy*, the era of U.S. Navy fossil fuel aircraft carriers will draw to a close. *U.S. Navy*

A NUCLEAR
AGE NAVY

A Nuclear Age Navy

Nuclear-powered warships rank with steam power, the screw drive, and all of the great inventions that enable navies to defeat their enemies. The U.S. Navy began its nuclear-power program in earnest, and it was first utilized aboard submarines with the USS *Nautilus* (SSN-571). This boat was commissioned on January 21, 1954, with scores of nuclear-powered submarines in a variety of classes to follow. Surface ships followed suit, yet not on a huge scale. In actuality, the cruisers, frigates, and destroyers totaled a mere nine vessels, and by the end of the twentieth century, all had been inactivated and broken up for scrap. The navy discovered that the submarine and super aircraft carrier were the most cost-efficient vessels to be considered for nuclear power.

The first of the nuclear super giants was the USS *Enterprise* (CVN-65), which was commissioned on November 25, 1961, and with the exception of overhauls and nuclear refueling, has been continuously operational for 48 years.

The next class of nuclear-powered aircraft carriers began with the USS *Nimitz* (CVN-68) when it was commissioned on March 3, 1975. The USS *Dwight D. Eisenhower* (CVN-69) and USS *Carl Vinson* (CVN-70) followed on its heels and were all *Nimitz*-class carriers. The last of the group (*Carl Vinson*) came online in 1982. The next group of nuclear carriers began with the USS *Theodore Roosevelt* (CVN-71), which was commissioned on October 25, 1986—more than ten years since the *Nimitz* joined the fleet.

The next offering in American naval aviation at sea will be the futuristic carrier that has been the subject of speculation in naval aviation communities worldwide. This is the CVN-21 or twenty-first-century nuclear carrier. Of course, from a practical standpoint, the carrier is now simply designated

Previous page: The second of the *Nimitz*-class nuclear carriers, the USS *George Washington* (CVN-69) plows thousands of tons of water off her bow while transiting the Atlantic. *U.S. Navy*

CVN-78, the carrier hull number after the USS *George H. W. Bush* (CVN-77). This carrier will likely be much like its predecessor in overall appearance; however, the systems within the hull will be far more advanced and heavily reliant on electricity.

A major development at the dawn of the twenty-first century for the U.S. Navy is the elimination of a number of different aircraft from its inventory. The popular and near-cult favorite F-14 Tomcat has been retired, and the S-3 Viking is also on the chopping block. Replacing these aircraft will be the F/A-18E/F Super Hornet and the revolutionary F-35C Joint Strike Fighter. The primary electronic jamming aircraft aboard the carriers, the EA-6B Prowler, will soon be replaced by the EA-18G. In terms of command and control, the E-2

The ultramodern USS *Ronald Reagan* (CVN-76) and sister nuclear giant, USS *Abraham Lincoln* (CVN-72), operate in the Pacific with the oldest: the fossil fuel–powered USS *Kitty Hawk* (CV-63). The *Kitty Hawk* will soon be retired to a boneyard. *U.S. Navy*

The USS *Carl Vinson* (CVN-70), one of the earlier *Nimitz* nuclear-class supercarriers, leaves San Diego in February 2005. The *Vinson* was based at North Island. *Author's collection*

The USS *Abraham Lincoln* (CVN-72), a more modern *Nimitz* class, sits in dry-dock in Bremerton, Washington. Actually, it is the Bravo Pier at the Kitsap Naval Base shipyard. The carrier was in for a general overhaul in May 2004. *Author's collection*

The USS *Harry S. Truman* (CVN-75), a very modern *Theodore Roosevelt* subclass of the *Nimitz* nuclear carriers, speeds across the Atlantic. *U.S. Navy*

Hawkeye has been in the sky over the fleet or near combat areas since 1973. The navy is testing a vastly improved Hawkeye (E-2D) with ADS-18 electronically scanned array radar.

In addition, the Osprey and Harrier have been joined by unmanned aircraft such as the RQ-4 Global Hawk, the RQ-8A, and MQ-8B Fire Scout. The day of having a diverse air group composed of fighters, strike fighters, bombers, ASW specialists, reconnaissance, and "in flight" refuelers might have passed, but there will always be a place for land-based aviation to fill the gap in carrier strength.

An idyllic picture of an MH-60S Seahawk flying a pallet of ammunition from the nuclear carrier USS *Harry S. Truman* (CVN-75) to the USS *George Washington* (CVN-70) at sunset during an Atlantic crossing. *U.S. Navy*

USS *Enterprise* (CVN-65) was the first nuclear aircraft carrier built by any nation, and has many years left in its powerplant as well as its overall hull-technology systems. The ship stunned the world and, in particular, the Soviet Union—which was one of its designed purposes.

USS *ENTERPRISE*

Built by Newport News Shipyard and Dry-dock Corporation in Newport News, Virginia

Commissioned: November 25, 1961, after being laid down on February 4, 1958

Full-load displacement: 104,000 tons

Length: 1,123 feet; Beam: (flight deck) 252 feet

Propulsion: eight A2W reactors and four steam turbines turning four propellers; four emergency generators producing 10,270 horsepower; shaft horsepower is 280,000

Top speed: 30-plus knots

Armament: two Sea Sparrow launchers; two RAM (rolling airframe) launchers; three 20mm Phalanx CIWS; variety of 50mm and 60mm machine guns to ward off attack by boarders, suicide boats, and the like

Crew: 3,500; with an air wing of 2,480

Aircraft capacity: eighty-five consisting of the F-35C Joint Strike Fighter; F/A-18 Hornet; EA-6B Prowlers, and a number of E-2C Hawkeyes

Note: There are also an unknown number of UAVs aboard or planned for. The typical air group is seventy-two fixed wing and six to eight rotary wing aircraft. The *Enterprise* will be replaced by CVN-78 in 2018.

On October 13, 2005, an F/A-18C Hornet is towed into the hangar of the USS *Harry S. Truman* (CVN-75). All important carrier qualifications are being done aboard the *Truman* off the United States' East Coast. *U.S. Navy*

USS *Nimitz* (CVN-68), the second of the nuclear supercarriers, slowly steams into San Francisco for Fleet Week in October 2006. The *Nimitz* was the first of ten ships in the class built at the Newport News Shipyard and Dry-dock Corporation at Newport News, Virginia. The last is the USS *George H. W. Bush* (CVN-77) christened October 7, 2006.

USS *NIMITZ*
Built by Newport News Shipyard and Dry-dock Corporation in Newport News, Virginia
Commissioned: May 3, 1975
Full-load displacement: 101,000 to 104,000 tons
Length: 1,092 feet; Beam: on flight deck 252 feet
Propulsion: two Westinghouse A4W nuclear reactors connected to four steam turbines generating 260,000 shaft horsepower; ship should steam fifteen years without refueling; four emergency diesel generators producing 10,270 horsepower
Top speed: 30-plus knots
Armament: two rolling airframe missile systems (twenty-one missiles), three 20mm Phalanx CIWS, two Mark 29 Sea Sparrow batteries
Crew: 3,200; with an air group of 2,480
Aircraft capacity: ninety fixed and rotary wing aircraft, yet the typical air group is seventy-two fixed wing and six to eight rotary wing aircraft
Note: The *Nimitz* is expected to be in service through 2033.

March 19, 2005, and the USS *Carl Vinson* (CVN-70) relieves the nuclear carrier USS *Harry S. Truman* (CVN-75) for duty in the Persian Gulf. *U.S. Navy*

The USS *John C. Stennis* (CVN-74) operates off the southern California coast. The *Stennis* is part of the *Theodore Roosevelt* subclass, and one of its less obvious but more effective improvements is the removal of more than 5,900 tons of heavy armor. In lieu of armor, the carrier was built with a double hull, which tests have proven will reduce the damage of torpedoes. The USS *Stennis* strike group, with more than 6,500 sailors and marines, entered the Persian Gulf in late March 2007 along with the guided-missile cruiser USS *Antietam*. The *Stennis* joined the strike group led by the carrier USS *Dwight D. Eisenhower*, the first time two U.S. aircraft carriers have operated in the Gulf since the U.S.-led invasion of Iraq in 2003. *U.S. Navy*

USS *THEODORE ROOSEVELT*

Built by Newport News Shipyard and Dry-dock, Newport News, Virginia

Commissioned: October 25, 1981

Full-load displacement: 101,000 to 104,000 tons

Length: 1,092 feet; Beam: 252 feet at the widest point on the flight deck

Propulsion: Westinghouse A4W nuclear reactors; four steam turbines with fifteen years between refueling; four emergency diesel engines producing 10,270 horsepower

Propulsion: 260,000 shaft horsepower

Top speed: 30-plus knots

Armament: NATO Sea Sparrow missiles, 20mm Phalanx CIWS, rolling airframe (RAM) system with twenty-one missiles

Crew: 3,200; with an air group of 2,480

Aircraft capacity: eighty, although a typical air group consists of seventy-two fixed wing and six-to eight rotary wing aircraft

Note: The ship should be a fleet unit through 2038.

Opposite page: The USS *Theodore Roosevelt* (CVN-71) is different in so many ways from the *Nimitz* that it is regarded as a separate class, or subclass. In this March 10, 2006, image, the ship launches its last F-14D Tomcats as they depart for Oceana Naval Air Station (NAS) and then squadron decommissioning.

On May 14, 2006, the USS *Ronald Reagan* (CVN-76) passes Palm Island to enter Jebel-Ali on the transit to oil-wealthy nations of the United Arab Emirates. This manmade island in the shape of the ever-present desert palm tree is reflective of the wealth available in certain nations in the Near East. Aside from the carrier strike group, there are local escorts. The *Reagan* will take up maritime security operations (MSO) in the region. *U.S. Navy*

The building sequence of the last of the *Nimitz*-class nuclear carriers: (CVN-77) or the USS *George H. W. Bush*. The first modular section is laid at Northrop Grumman on September 6, 2003. *U.S. Navy*

USS *Ronald Reagan* (CVN-76) looks slightly different from its predecessors and the interior systems are more reliant on electrical output. Consequently, the *Reagan* is regarded as its own class.

USS *Ronald Reagan*
Built by Newport News Shipyard and Dry-dock, Newport News, Virginia
Commissioned: July 12, 2003
Full-load displacement: up to 104,000 tons
Length: 1,092 feet; Beam: 252 feet at flight deck (maximum)
Propulsion: two Westinghouse A4W nuclear reactors and can operate fifteen years between refueling. The shaft horsepower is 260,000, which can drive the ship at speeds in excess of thirty knots on a sustained basis. The ship carries four diesel powerplants that generate 10,270 horsepower for emergencies. Armament: the evolved Sea Sparrow missile (ESSM); 20mm Phalanx CIWS, and the twenty-one missile rolling airframe (RAM)
Crew: 3,200; with an air wing of 2,480
Note: The *Reagan* can embark up to ninety aircraft; however, the typical air group is seventy-two fixed wing and six to eight rotary wing aircraft. It should serve the fleet for a minimum of a half century or up through 2053.

Early 2005 and the hull, internal structure, and the bulbous bow of the *Bush* is taking shape. *U.S. Navy*

Paint does wonders: the CVN-77 is about ready for christening with its name, the USS *George H. W. Bush*. The lower sections of the ship are prepared for the dry-dock to be flooded and allow the great ship to take on life. A month later, the dry-dock was flooded and the ship floated without incident. It was formally christened on October 7, 2006. There are many months remaining before this carrier can go to sea as an active fleet unit. *U.S. Navy*

USS *George H. W. Bush* is the precursor to the CVN-21 or CVN-78, as many of its systems will be the same as those aboard the newest and most revolutionary carrier now being designed.

USS *GEORGE H. W. BUSH*

Built in Newport News, Virginia, by the Northrop Grumman Newport News Shipyard (the successor to the Newport News Shipyard and Dry-dock Company)

Commissioned: tentative; scheduled for 2009 (the ship was christened October 7, 2007)

Full-load displacement: 104,000-plus tons

Length: 1,092 feet; Beam: 252 feet at the widest point on the flight deck

Propulsion: two Westinghouse A4D nuclear reactors driving four steam turbines; the powerplant generates 260,000 shaft horsepower

Top speed: 30-plus knots (sustained)

Armament: three Phalanx 20mm CIWS, two Mark 29 Sea Sparrow batteries, two rolling airframe missile systems (twenty-one missiles)

Crew: 3,200; with an air wing of 2,480

Aircraft capacity: ninety; however, the typical air group consists of seventy-two fixed wing and six to eight rotary wing aircraft. This can change due to different mission packages. The *George H. W. Bush* should be a viable U.S. Navy asset until 2059.

The successor to the *Nimitz* class and its subclasses, the much-heralded CVN-21 (twenty-first-century nuclear carrier) or more properly, CVN-78. The ship is still in its design and conceptual stage, but it will probably rely heavily on electrical output to operate its hundreds of motors to replace sailors and staff hours. *U.S. Navy*

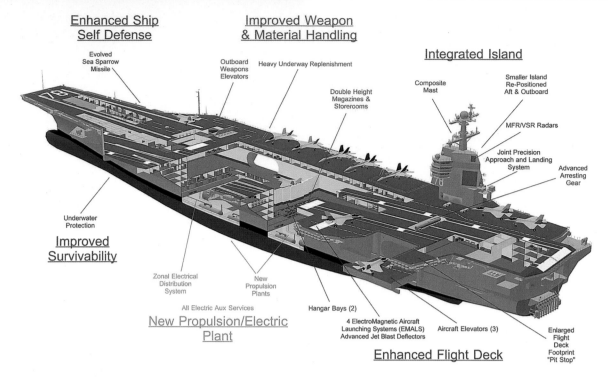

Enhanced Ship Self Defense
- Evolved Sea Sparrow Missile

Improved Weapon & Material Handling
- Outboard Weapons Elevators
- Heavy Underway Replenishment
- Double Height Magazines & Storerooms

Integrated Island
- Composite Mast
- Smaller Island Re-Positioned Aft & Outboard
- MFR/VSR Radars
- Joint Precision Approach and Landing System
- Advanced Arresting Gear

Improved Survivability
- Underwater Protection

New Propulsion/Electric Plant
- Zonal Electrical Distribution System
- New Propulsion Plants
- All Electric Aux Services

Enhanced Flight Deck
- Hangar Bays (2)
- 4 ElectroMagnetic Aircraft Launching Systems (EMALS) Advanced Jet Blast Deflectors
- Aircraft Elevators (3)
- Enlarged Flight Deck Footprint "Pit Stop"

USS *Gerald R. Ford*
Grumman Newport News Shipyard,
　　Newport News, Virginia
Commissioned: due in 2015
Full-load displacement: will likely be more than
　　100,000 tons, and the dimensions the same
　　as CVN-77
Top speed: in excess of 30 knots on a sustained
　　basis
Armament: evolved Sea Sparrow, rolling
　　airframe missiles, and 20mm Phalanx CIWS
　　Crew (including air wing): 4,660 (one
　　thousand less than *Nimitz* [CVN-68])
Aircraft capacity: seventy-five-plus aircraft;
　　including the F-35C JSF; F/A-18E/F, EA-18G,
　　E-2D, MH-60R/S, and J-UCAS (joint
　　unmanned combat air system)
Note: A new nuclear reactor will be utilized; the
　　AIB, and stealthier overall features will help
　　reduce the radar signature of the ship. The
　　ship should go without refueling for almost
　　half of its life (twenty-five years). *Ford*
　　should be a fleet unit well into the late 2060s.

Currently in design, the CVN-78 will revolutionize naval aviation at sea. This ship and those in this entirely new class will continually be upgradeable without the telltale marks, overwelds, and alterations that mark them as ships that have been changed over and over. Electrical output will be triple that of previous nuclear carriers, and equipment for launching and recovery will heavily depend on all-new electrical systems. As of 2006, three of the class are planned (CVN-78, CVN-79, and CVN-80); however, an additional seven might be progressively funded and built into 2026 to replace the *Nimitz* class.

A three-image sequence of how to get an aircraft back aboard a moving aircraft carrier. This World War II landing signal officer (LSO) stands in front of a tarp shield and waves his paddles aboard the escort carrier USS *Charger* (CVE-30) to guide an incoming aircraft. *Author's collection*

The Fresnel landing signal lights aboard a nuclear carrier are being adjusted by a technician. They are part of a complex system to reduce recovery errors and fatalities. *U.S. Navy*

Naval aviators serve as judges of their shipmates who are attempting to land in perfect fashion. They control a "pickle stick" that can cause the system to waive the pilot off, and automatically give a poor grade, something no aspiring pilot wants. These LSOs are aboard the USS *Theodore Roosevelt*. The improved Fresnel lens optical landing system (IFLOLS) will soon be installed aboard all carriers in the fleet. *U.S. Navy*

The F/A-18C and F/A-18E's armament features 20mm M61A1/A2 Vulcan cannon external pods with up to 17,750 pounds of weaponry, including nearly all of the U.S. Navy's bombs, rockets, and missiles.

F/A-18C F/A-18E "HORNET"
Built by Boeing Aircraft
Country: United States
Powerplant: two GE F414-GE-400 turbofans
Top speed: mach 1.8
Range: 681 miles
Service ceiling: 50,000 feet

The supercarriers as well as all surface ships, including the big-deck amphibious carriers, need a smaller vessel to train rotary wing pilots. The 500-ton, 125-foot-long-by-36-foot-wide helicopter landing trainer (HLT-1 or IX-514) provided the perfect craft. Acquired and refitted in 1986, [the HLT has not had an accident in more than 100,000 landings by novice pilots. The HLT-1 is home ported at the Pensacola Naval Air Station. *U.S. Navy*

Aircraft engines are tested off the stern of carriers such as the *Kitty Hawk*. The ship's name is well lit by the jet engine exhaust from an F/A-18C *Hornet*. *U.S. Navy*

The eight-year-old USS *Langley* (CV-1) is moored near the same location as the *Nimitz* in this 1930 photo. An all-gun light cruiser, the USS *Omaha* (CL-4) is anchored in the harbor. Japanese aircraft sunk the *Langley* in February 1942, and the *Omaha* was scrapped after World War II. *Author's collection*

The F-35C will have a larger, folding wing and larger control surfaces for improved low-speed control, and stronger landing gear for the stresses of carrier landings. The larger wing area provides increased range and payload, with twice the range on internal fuel compared with the F/A-18C, achieving much the same goal as the much heavier Super Hornet. A GAU-12/U 25mm cannon will be mounted internally, and it will be able to carry a variety of missiles.

F-35C JOINT STRIKE FIGHTER
Built by Lockheed Martin
Country: United States
Powerplant: Pratt & Whitney F135 afterburning turbofan
Top speed: mach 1.6
Range: 620 miles
Service ceiling: 48,000 feet

The Naval Air Station at North Island in San Diego Bay. The USS *Ronald Reagan* is just tying up as thousands of loved ones wait to see the husbands, wives, sisters, and so forth that make up the crew. In the background is the first of the *Nimitz* class, the USS *Nimitz* (CVN-68). It has become a common sight to see nuclear carriers come and go from this port. *U.S. Navy*

The USS *George Washington* (CVN-73) begins the dry-dock process by entering the dock. Soon, the caisson doors will close behind the 100,000-ton carrier, and once it is properly set, the water will be drained. Work can then safely begin on the outer hull. *U.S. Navy*

The U.S. Naval Base at Subic Bay in the Philippines. Across the bay is the Cubi Point Naval Air Station where carriers ranging from the older *Essex* class to the modern supercarriers could moor during the Vietnam War. *U.S. Navy*

The AV-8B Harrier II jets are assigned to the "Bulldogs" of Marine Attack Squadron 223. They can be launched from virtually any location depending on variation. Each features a GAU-12/U equalizer 25mm cannon plus seven pylons for 13,200 pounds of other weapons.

AV-8B HARRIER II
Built by BAE Systems/Boeing Aircraft
Country: United Kingdom/United States
Powerplant: Rolls-Royce F402-RR-408
Top speed: 675 mph
Range: 1,200 nautical miles
Service ceiling: 50,000 feet

A few of the former *Essex*-class aircraft carriers such as the USS *Hornet* (CV-12) located in Alameda, California, have found homes as museum ships. A total of four *Essex*-class carriers have become quite popular museum ships on all of the U.S. coasts. Most have the type of aircraft flown from their decks as static displays. *Author's collection, by Melissa Lanzaro*

The end of the line for many of the older carriers. This is the Inactive Ships Maintenance Site at Puget Sound (Kitsap) in Bremerton, Washington. There are other sites around the United States for supercarriers such as the former USS *Ranger* (CV-61), USS *Independence* (CV-62), and the USS *Constellation* (CV-64). A decision must be made as to their future disposition. *Author's collection*

The E-2 Hawkeye reconnaissance aircraft is the "eye in the sky" for the carrier battle group. The latest version can track two thousand targets simultaneously (while at the same time, detecting twenty thousand simultaneously) to a range greater than four hundred miles (650 km) and simultaneously guide forty to one hundred intercepts.

E-2 HAWKEYE
Built by Northrop Grumman
Country: United States
Powerplant: two Allison
**   T56 turboprops**
Top speed: 375 mph
Range: 1,605 miles
Service ceiling: 30,800 feet
Armament: nil

A daylight shot of an MH-60S Seahawk transferring ammunition from one carrier to another. Here a *Bay Raiders* helo from the HSC-28 Sea Combat Squadron returns an ammunition pallet from the USS *Harry S. Truman* (CVN-75) to the USS *Dwight D. Eisenhower* (CVN-69). Training on some of the most mundane tasks pays off in the long run. *U.S. Navy*

Opposite page bottom: Many of the older carriers have become artificial reefs, including the former USS *Oriskany* (CV-34) being sunk off the Florida coast in the spring of 2006. There were a lot of tears on May 17, 2006, as the ten preset explosives opened the very popular ship to the ocean. Thirty-seven minutes later, the ship foundered and a few minutes later it was resting upright in 212 feet of water. A fish and diver paradise. *U.S. Navy*

P-3C Orion
Built by Lockheed
Country: United States
Powerplant: four T6 A-14
           Allison turboprops
Top speed: 411 knots
Range: 1,345 miles
Service ceiling: 27,000

The P-3C Orion maritime patrol, reconnaissance, and antisubmarine aircraft's armament includes ASW torpedoes, mines, depth charges, and harpoon missiles. *U.S. Navy*

One of the most popular aircraft in the U.S. Navy: the F-14 Tomcat. The Tomcats were officially retired in September 2006, yet this pilot could not resist the urge to do a close flyby over the USS *Theodore Roosevelt* (CVN-71). *U.S. Navy*

The A-3B Skywarrior twin-engine carrier attack aircraft was introduced in 1955 to carry two atomic bombs to targets in the Soviet Union or Soviet Bloc nations. It had a range of 2,360 miles at 459 knots and carried two 2,025-pound weapons. This aircraft was filmed at the Pima Museum in Tucson, Arizona. *Author's collection*

The COD (carrier onboard delivery): the twin-piston-engine aircraft is a C-2A Greyhound that delivers personnel and supplies out as far as 1,300 miles. It is the primary shuttle aircraft that can fly at three-hundred-plus knots per hour. *U.S. Navy*

The SH-60 Seahawk is an attack and general-purpose helicopter used in antisubmarine warfare, missile targeting, antiship attack, search and rescue, strike warfare, and VIP transport. Nations/organizations using the Seahawk or its variants include the U.S. Coast Guard (Jayhawk), U.S. Marine Corps, U.S. Army (Black Hawk), Turkey, Spain, Japan, Australia, Taiwan, Greece, and Thailand.

SH-60 SEAHAWK
Built by Sikorsky
Country: United States
Powerplant: two 1260 KW GE T700-GE-401C
    turboshaft engines
Top speed: 145 mph
Range: 380 miles
Service ceiling: 19,000 feet

The A-6 Intruder has had many variations since being introduced to naval aviation. It has been the primary all-weather day-or-night bomber since the days of the Vietnam War. It is capable of 571 knots or 412 knots cruising speed. Its bomb load is phenomenal, and it has fought its way through one war after another with honors and the ability to take punishment. It is now retired. *U.S. Navy*

The Blue Angels have used nine different aircraft over six decades as the U.S. Navy's flight exhibition team, including a specialized C-130 Hercules named "Fat Albert" to carry spares and so forth. They perform for nearly fifteen million spectators per year, with close to four hundred million since 1946. Twenty-five Blue Angel pilots and enlisted aircrew have perished during more than six decades of flight exhibitions and training. *U.S. Navy*

The world-famous Blue Angels, the U.S. Navy's flight exhibition team, performs one of its routines ("fleur-de-lis," or flower of lily). Beginning in 1946 with the propeller-driven F6F-5 Hellcat of World War II carrier-battle fame, the Blues have flown nine different aircraft culminating with the F/A-18A Hornet. *U.S. Navy*

BLUE ANGELS
Aircraft currently in use: F/A-18A Hornet
Built by Boeing Aircraft
Top speed: mach 1.8 or 1,127 mph
Service ceiling: 50,000 feet
First aircraft: F6F-5 Hellcat. This was a propeller-driven aircraft of great fame in the Pacific War.
Date began: May 10, 1946
First jet aircraft: F9F-2 "Panther" 1949 to June 1950

An EA-6B Prowler launches off a nuclear carrier. Its task is to protect the task force and ground troops by jamming enemy radar, data links, and overall communications. It has a range of more than one thousand nautical miles and speeds of five-hundred-plus knots. Despite its excellent performance, it will soon be phased out and replaced. *U.S. Navy*

The T-45A Goshawk training jet is capable of 645 miles per hour with a range of 700 nautical miles. It is the primary jet trainer for pilot training. *U.S. Navy*

The use of unmanned aerial vehicles (UAVs) like the Fire Scout (shown) and Global Hawk aboard aircraft carriers has been under study.

GLOBAL HAWK AND FIRE SCOUT
Both the Global Hawk and the Fire Scout have the capability of reconnaissance, attack with missiles, and loitering over a target area for a number of hours. This enables intelligence to be relayed back to the fleet.

The most famous SB-3 Viking in the U.S. Navy is about to be trapped on the USS *Abraham Lincoln* (CVN-72) off the Pacific Coast. This twin-engine jet aircraft was used to detect and destroy enemy submarines during the Cold War beginning in 1975. "Navy 1" was occupied and flown by President George W. Bush and safely landed on May 1, 2003, during his much-discussed symbolic gesture in celebration of Operation Iraqi Freedom's early successes ("Mission Accomplished"). This Viking was flown to Pensacola to be placed on permanent display in the Naval Aviation Museum. The cockpit was quite crowded with President Bush, a navy pilot, and cameramen. *U.S. Navy*

FOREIGN NAVIES

Foreign Navies

Since the end of World War II, and later in the aftermath of the collapse of the Soviet Union, foreign naval aviation has moved through a metamorphosis. At first, nations that played a prominent military role in World War II attempted to maintain naval aviation at sea with their aircraft carriers. The ships and aircraft were chronologically new, but technologically obsolescing. The jet engine, radar, and atomic weapons had all but consigned these beautiful pieces of military hardware to the history books.

As the Cold War began to take its toll on the budgets of the Western powers and the Warsaw Pact nations, aircraft carriers slowly disappeared and were either scrapped or sold off to smaller nations in South America. By the end of the Cold War and collapse of the Soviet Union (1990), few nations had any real power projection at sea in the form of aircraft carriers. In fact, of all the naval aircraft at sea, less than 10 percent flew from aircraft carriers not flying the Stars and Stripes.

The U.S. Navy is the only force that continues to build the huge nuclear-powered aircraft carriers. Other nations quickly are acquiring smaller vessels that can manage up to thirty Joint Strike Fighters and powerful, special-mission helicopters. With the ability to launch aircraft without the expensive and flight deck–consuming catapults, the smaller carrier is becoming more popular. Eventually, any nation able to build amphibious warships with a large deck will be able to launch and recover powerful fighter-bombers.

The genesis of this change was in 1982 with the stunning success of Great Britain and its Sea Harriers and Sea King helicopters flying from smaller carriers in extremely poor weather conditions. Great Britain was compelled to regain its property from the invading Argentine military. For a lesser power, which was actually a client for much

Previous page: The V/STOL carrier HMS *Invincible* (R-05), which has been in Royal Navy service since July 11, 1980. It carries six Sea Harriers and seven Sea King helicopters. *U.S. Navy*

The fleet of tomorrow: multinational ships solve a maritime problem. Escorts and supply and replenishment ships accompany the carriers USS *John Stennis* (CVN-74), FS *Charles de Gaulle* (R-91), HMS *Ocean* (L-12), and USS *John F. Kennedy* (CV-67). This U.S. Navy photo was taken on April 18, 2002, in the Oman Sea during Operation Enduring Freedom. *U.S. Navy*

of the defense industry in England, to defeat Her Majesty's Forces was unthinkable. Unfortunately, Great Britain had little in the way of assets to move its army and marines a great distance from their homeland to fight. Taking a chance on the smaller jump jet carriers and Sea Harrier aircraft, the Royal Navy and forces on the ground soundly smashed the Argentine military that depended on conventional naval aircraft that were land based in Argentina. They also had the dreaded Exocet antiship missile that turned out to be devastating to escorts in the Royal Navy.

It was unnecessary to launch dozens of aircraft to do the job of less than forty Sea Harriers with their improved weaponry and tactics. This has been strongly reinforced over the last several years and in particular in the Middle East. Accurate missiles, bombs, and rockets have negated the need for carpet bombing and dozens of aircraft that once were needed to achieve what a very few can

do right now. This means smaller numbers of carrier-type ships and aircraft. This also means that littoral warfare is the new battleground for navies.

Maritime strikes; littoral maneuvers; and command, control, and protection of access to the beach and beachheads will be the primary goals of aircraft carriers operating in the littoral. Secondary roles will include defense diplomacy, humanitarian assistance, disaster relief, and evacuation of citizens from endangered areas.

Naval aviation in the twenty-first century will still exist, yet on a global basis. More nations will field aircraft carrier–type ships with aircraft that are made for the new century. Even container ships with welded plating along the sides to form a protective bulkhead for aircraft being carried could be considered aircraft carriers. The key will be improved technology that will continue to be refined and built with greater cost-consciousness.

This 1991 photo shows four aircraft carriers/amphibious carriers (back to front): HMS *Invincible* (R-05), USS *Forrestal* (CV-59), USS *Wasp* (LHD-1), and SPS *Principe de Asturias* (R-11). *U.S. Navy*

HMS *INVINCIBLE*
(light V/STOL carrier)
Full-load displacement: **20,600 tons**
Length: **685 feet**
Top speed: **28 knots**
Aircraft capacity: up to sixteen Sea
     Harriers/Harriers and four helicopters

USS *FORRESTAL*
(Supercarrier)
See Chapter 1

USS *WASP*
(amphibious assult carrier)
Full-load displacement: **40,522 tons**
Length: **844 feet**
Top speed: **22 knots**
Aircraft capacity: eight AV-8B Harriers
     with up to twenty additional or
     forty-two CH-46E Sea Knights and
     other helos

SPS *PRINCIPE DE ASTURIAS*
Full-load displacement: **17,188 tons**
Length: **643 feet**
Top speed: **25 knots**
Aircraft capacity: twelve AV-8B Harriers,
     eight Sea King helos

HMS *Illustrious* (R-06), which entered Royal Navy service on June 20, 1982. It is quite similar to the *Invincible*, and both will be replaced by the HMS *Queen Elizabeth* and HMS *Prince of Wales* in the near future. *U.S. Navy*

Two EH101 Merlin helicopters return from a training role in antisubmarine warfare. These aircraft are primarily for ASW and antisurface ship warfare. Accordingly, they carry four ASW homing torpedoes; two long-range missiles and depth bombs. *Royal Navy*

The CVF or CVH V/STOL carriers HMS *Queen Elizabeth* and HMS *Prince of Wales* are in design stage in Great Britain. They are intended to replace HMS *Invincible* and HMS *Illustrious*. The cost for both carriers is expected to be $7.6 billion. *Royal Navy*

HMS *QUEEN ELIZABETH/PRINCE OF WALES*
Not yet built (currently in the design stage)
Commissioned: 2015 and 2018, respectively
Full-load displacement: 50,000 tons
Length: 951 feet; Beam: 272 feet on flight deck
Propulsion: four Rolls-Royce gas turbine
    engines; 100,000 shaft horsepower
Top speed: 28 knots
Armament: unknown
Aircraft capacity: forty-eight aircraft, including thirty-eight Joint
    Strike Fighters F-35B and ten helicopters

The newly acquired aircraft carrier *NAe Sao Paulo* (A-12). In 2000, Brazil purchased this *Clemenceau*-class 32,800-ton full-load carrier from France where it was known as the *Foch* as originally commissioned in 1960. From Kuwait, Brazil purchased twenty-three Skyhawk fighter-bombers, which will constitute the core of the ship's air group. *Author's collection*

One of the primary designs for Great Britain's sixty-thousand-ton full-load aircraft carrier HMS *Queen Elizabeth* or HMS *Prince of Wales*. This will be a departure from the twenty-thousand-ton types built in the 1980s, and will be the CVF carrier of the future. The F-35 Lightning II is easily identifiable on the flight deck as is the Merlin helicopter. *U.S. Navy*

The former small or CVL carrier, RAN *Sydney*. It was a World War II *Colossus*-class carrier that served many commonwealth of other navies before the entire class was retired due to age and lack of modern technology. *Author's collection*

The F-35 Lightning II's armament will include a GAU-12/U 25mm cannon plus up to four guided bombs, Sidewinder missiles, and other weapons carried internally or on externally mounted pods. *U.S. Navy*

F-35 LIGHTNING II
Lockheed Martin fighter aircraft
Grants Naval Aviation Program superiority
Produced by Lockheed Martin in the United States
Powerplant: a Pratt & Whitney F135 afterburning turbofan
Top speed: 1,200 miles per hour
Range: 1,200 nautical miles
Service ceiling: unknown as yet

The Italian carrier MM *Giuseppe Garibaldi* at sea. It is 13,850 tons full load and entered fleet service in 1983. *Author's collection*

A Brazilian Skyhawk is launched off the *Sao Paulo*. *Author's collection*

The French navy's CVN *Charles de Gaulle* is the first nuclear aircraft carrier in Western Europe, and due to the problems with this system, probably the last. The French are not planning to build another carrier that will be dependent on nuclear power. *U.S. Navy*

CVN *CHARLES DE GAULLE*
Built by DCN, Brest, France
Commissioned: May 18, 2001
Full-load displacement: 40,400 tons
Length: 857.7 feet; Beam: 211.3 feet
   (flight deck)
Propulsion: nuclear power 83,000 shaft
   horsepower
Top speed: 25.2 knots
Armament: surface-to-air missiles
Aircraft capacity: ten Rafale fighters, sixteen
   to twenty Super Etendard strike fighters
   and various helicopters

The Dassault Super Etendard French strike fighter. It has a maximum speed of 733 miles per hour and a range of 2,300 miles. It carries a combination of bombs, rockets, and the Exocet antiship missile. It will be replaced in the near future by the navalized Rafale. *U.S. Navy*

The SNS *Dedalo* or the former USS *Cabot* (CVL-28). The *Dedalo* was a light carrier in the Spanish Navy for several years after purchase from the United States. It carries a mix of helicopters and a Matador jump jet (similar to the Sea Harrier). It was returned to the United States in 1989 to become a museum ship; however, the venture was an abject failure. *Author's collection*

The SPS *Principe de Asturias* (R-11) has a 12-degree ski jump used for a variety of tasks: protection of coastal areas, sea control, maritime protection, and limited warfare. It replaced the SNS *Dedalo*, a converted former U.S. Navy light carrier, USS *Cabot* CVL-28 (circa World War II). *U.S. Navy*

SPS *PRINCIPE DE ASTURIAS*
Built by Izar, Ferrol, Spain
Commissioned: May 30, 1988
Full-load displacement: 17,188 tons
Length: 640 feet; Beam: 98.4 feet (flight deck)
Propulsion: two GE IM-2500 gas turbines, one controllable pitch propeller
Top speed: 26 knots
Armament: four twelve-barrel 20mm Meroka CIWS
  Aircraft capacity: six to eight Sea Harriers and up to sixteen helicopters

The Spanish carrier SPS *Principe de Asturias* (R-11), a ski ramp carrier that carries Matadors and helicopters. It displaces 13,400 tons and has been used in a variety of roles. *Author's collection*

The *Principe de Asturias* launches a Matador while on NATO maneuvers. *U.S. Navy*

The sun sets as the small task force moves onward. The small Spanish carrier is to the far left. All activities at night aboard a warship are not without some beauty. Seamen aboard the ships occasionally pause to look at a beautiful sky. Unfortunately, during wartime, this is the most dangerous time of the day, as submarines choose this time to attack and elude escorts. *U.S. Navy*

The Spanish Navy's EAV-8B Matador II is the primary fighter/fighter-bomber carried aboard the *Principe de Asturias* (R-11). Its armament includes one GAU–12/U equalizer 25mm cannon. *Author's collection*

EAV-8B MATADOR II
Built by BAE/Boeing Aircraft
United Kingdom/United States
Propulsion: Rolls-Royce—Pegasus 105
        vectored thrust turbofan
Top speed: 675 mph
Range: 1,200 nautical miles
Service ceiling: 50,000 feet
Crew: 1
Aircraft capacity: seven pylons for various
        other weapons, bombs, missiles, etc.

The ex-Soviet carrier *Minsk*, now the property of a cartel of Chinese entrepreneurs. They have created an amusement park called Minsk World on the highway leading to Beijing. The park is facing bankruptcy as of late 2006. *Author's collection*

The MiG-29 Fulcrum, a popular aircraft in the Indian, Chinese, and Russian navies. While no match for an F/A-18 Hornet, it is a credible fighter-bomber. *Author's collection*

Spain's *Buque de Proyeccion Estrategica* strategic projection carrier was to have been the "sea control" ship of the late 1980s; it was designed in the United States but never built. It will probably be commissioned as the *Juan Carlos I* in honor of the present monarch. The *Juan Carlos* will work in tandem with Spain's other carrier and surface escorts. It will also serve as an LHD (helicopter assault ship) and amphibious ship and carry up to four LCU landing craft in a well deck. The deck opens via a stern gate. Nine hundred troops can be accommodated aboard this new ship. *U.S. Navy*

BUQUE DE PROYECCION ESTRATEGICA
Built by Navantia (formerly Izar shipyards, Ferrol, Spain)
Commissioned: prospectively 2008
Full-load displacement: 27,079 tons
Length: 757 feet; Beam: 105 feet (flight deck)
Propulsion: gas turbine—azipods
Top speed: 21 knots
Brake horsepower: 34,872
Armament: four 20mm CIWS and RAM (rolling airframe missile)
Aircraft capacity: thirty V/STOL (Sea Harrier, Rafale fighters, Joint Strike Fighters) plus a variety of rotary wing aircraft

Another popular aircraft is the Lynx helicopter, which has just emerged from the aft deck of the Dutch guided-missile frigate HLMS *De Zeven Provincien* F-802. The helo, utilized on small carriers all over Europe, is rugged and dependable. One of its primary assignments is ASW. *Author's collection*

An Indian Navy Sea Harrier Mk 51, T Mk 60 from the carrier, INS *Viraat*. The Sea Harrier uses a Rolls-Royce Pegasus Mark 105 vectored thrust turbofan. The thrust is 21,750 pounds. The maximum speed of the Sea Harrier is 575 knots and it cruises at 420 knots. *U.S. Navy*

Italy's *Cavour*-class V/STOL carrier is designed to work with Western navies and protect home shores. The MM *Cavour* (first ship) will ensure maritime safety for commercial vessels. *U.S. Navy*

CAVOUR CLASS
Built by Fincantieri, Muggiano, la Spezia
Commissioned: 2007
Full-load displacement: 26,500 tons
Length: 768 feet; Beam: 128 feet
Propulsion: gas turbines—diesel-electric 118,000 shaft horsepower
Top speed: 28-plus knots
Armament: surface-to-air missiles, two 76mm/.62-caliber OTO Melara super compact DP guns, three 25mm/.87-caliber Oerlikon weapons, four fixed 324mm ASW triple tubes with impact torpedoes
Aircraft capacity: eight AV-8B Harrier or twelve EH-101 helicopters or a mix of both

The forward deck of the INS *Viraat*. The larger helo is an advanced light helicopter (ALH) and the smaller rotary wing is a Chetak multipurpose helicopter. The Chetak is being upgraded with a new engine and likely will be called the Chetan. Both helos are well suited to carrier operations. *U.S. Navy.*

The *Admiral Kuznetsov*–class heavy aircraft carrier (CV) at moderate speed. Despite not utilizing this ship more than one week out of a month due to lack of funds, the navy plans to re-embark on a two-carrier building program in the next two years. One of the fifty-thousand-ton ships will be deployed in the Pacific and the other in the Baltic. *U.S. Navy*

The Soviet *Kiev*-class aircraft carrier *Admiral Gorshkov* was commissioned on December 20, 1987. After the collapse of the Soviet government, arrangements were made to acquire the carrier by the Indian Navy (INS). During its lay-up in Russia, a massive eighteen-hour fire nearly decimated the ship. Finally, the burnt-out hulk was transferred to India in January 2004. After wholesale alterations are completed in 2008, the ship will be named INS *Vikramaditya*. The cost will be $500 to $700 million (U.S. dollars). The *Vikramaditya* will be shorn of most of its heavy missile and gun armament forward to allow for a larger flight deck. *Author's collection*

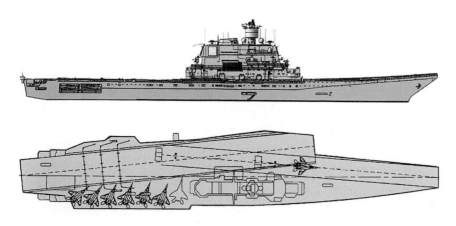

These drawings are of what the ship should resemble after completion of the shipyard work for the Indian Navy. *Author's collection*

13,500 トン型護衛艦   16 DDH

The Japanese DDH concept or helicopter-carrying destroyer. Rated at 13,500 tons, this helicopter carrier resembles a carrier far more than a destroyer. The Japanese Maritime Self Defense Force has planned four vessels (DDH-145–148). The ships are slated to carry three SH-60J Jayhawk helicopters (an export variant of the SH-60 Seahawk); however, the DDH is also armed with sixty-four cells capable of launching a variety of missiles and close-in weapons. *U.S. Navy*

The Royal Thailand aircraft carrier HTMS *Chakri Naruebet* is shown at sea with one of its six AV-8S Matador V/STOL fighters coming in to land. HTMS means "His Thai Majesty's Ship." *U.S. Navy*

HTMS *CHAKRI NARUEBET*
Built by Izar, Ferrol, Spain
Commissioned: August 10, 1997
Full-load displacement: 11,486 tons
Length: 599 feet; Beam: 100 feet (flight deck)
Propulsion: CODOG—two Bazan diesels and two GE IMS500
    gas turbines; 44,250 shaft horsepower
Top speed: 27.5 knots
Armament: yet to be installed due to lack of funding
    Aircraft capacity: six AV-8S Matador V/STOL fighters and
    four Seahawk helicopters; eighteen helicopters maximum

The naval shipyard in St. Petersburg, Russia. Much of the work is done in huge sheds to prevent observation by prying eyes (satellites), and to keep workers from freezing during winter months. The rather odd-looking ship with "770" written on it is a Zubr (Bison) air cushion landing craft (ACLC). The 770 is in the backwaters of St Petersburg, and there is no funding for completing this craft or others like it. *Author's collection*

The Rafale multirole combat fighter (Rafale M for marine version) is a twin-engine fighter that can be utilized on board an aircraft carrier or the ground. Its available armament includes four missiles, one 30mm cannon, and a variety of other weapons. *U.S. Navy*

RAFALE COMBAT FIGHTER
Built by Dassault
Country: France
Propulsion: two Snecma M88-2 E2 or E4 turbojets
Top speed: 1,450 mph
Range: 1,000 nautical miles
Service ceiling: 50,000 feet
Crew: 1

The Japanese DDH concept or helicopter-carrying destroyer. Rated at 13,500 tons, this helicopter carrier resembles a carrier far more than a destroyer. The Japanese Maritime Self Defense Force has planned four vessels (DDH-145–148). The ships are slated to carry three SH-60J Jayhawk helicopters (an export variant of the SH-60 Seahawk); however, the DDH is also armed with sixty-four cells capable of launching a variety of missiles and close-in weapons. *Author's collection*

AMPHIBIOUS WARFARE

Amphibious Warfare

Long before steam-powered ships and weapons depended on gunpowder, armies had to travel across oceans, lakes, and other bodies of water to attack their enemies. For hundreds of years, this approach to amphibious warfare continued almost unabated. Ultimately, it began to change, and by the beginning of the twentieth century, cruisers, battleships, and other larger ships would combine their marine contingents and a matching number of partially trained seamen to assault a particular beach, city, or land mass. This is what then constituted a landing force.

The large warships of the U.S. Navy employed its launches and liberty boats to transfer a composite landing force to the beach. Warships would stand off and cover the landing with their heavy guns, and communication was by semaphore or searchlights. In general, landing forces were never very large, organized, or well equipped. A squadron of battleships, cruisers, and torpedo boat destroyers would contribute less than a thousand men and arms that the men could carry. There was no doctrine that covered prelanding bombardment, and intelligence generally was derived from locals who came out to the ships with information (good, bad, or outright falsehoods). The landing force was indeed lucky not to be decimated during the time they were crawling over the sides of their boats, which were ground into the sand of an enemy shore. This scene was played out by most nations as none had really moved forward in amphibious doctrine. World War I began to cause some change as it was important to

Previous page: The USS *Thetis Bay* (CVE-90) an escort carrier which was launched March 16, 1944, is being overhauled at the San Francisco Naval Shipyard in 1956. The small carrier was being converted to a helicopter insertion carrier for the marines with a huge aircraft lift aft. It was originally classed as the CVHA-1, and later as LPH-6. The *Thetis Bay* acted as an excellent test bed for helicopter landing ships to come. *Author's collection*

August 20, 1937, in the Wangpo River, Shanghai, China. The U.S. Navy puts an amphibious landing force of armed seamen ashore to stop the artillery duel between Japanese and Chinese army batteries. A stray shell killed a sailor aboard the USS *Augusta* (CA-31), and the area was supposedly neutral. This was what amphibious tactics consisted of just prior to World War II. *Author's collection*

A tank landing ship (LST-325) makes its way back from Greece where it was a unit in the Royal Hellenic Navy from 1964 to 2000. The 328-foot-long craft was acquired by the USS LST Ship Memorial, and returned to the United States as a museum ship to honor the most important amphibious ship class of World War II. It was sailed on its own power by indomitable ex-LST sailors, and arrived home safely. *U.S. Navy*

bring thousands of troops from New Zealand, Australia, and the United States to the war zones in Europe and the Mediterranean region. Due to the need for men, the old ways would no longer work—men often were treated like cannon fodder on the fields of battle, but not aboard ships on the way to war.

Instead of crowded cargo ships where disease and unsanitary habits killed a percentage of the soldiers or marines, ships were designed to get men and women to the battle zone healthy and ready to carry out their mission. In days gone by, men who had been conscripted into a warlord's army had to travel by the crudest of means: slow, filthy, leaking, sailing, or coal-fired craft. Chinese warlords often utilized riverboats on the Yangtze River with standing room only for more than two thousand troops. On many

The USS *Thetis Bay* (CVE-90) an escort carrier which was launched March 16, 1944, is being overhauled at the San Francisco Naval Shipyard in 1956. The small carrier was being converted to a helicopter insertion carrier for the marines with a huge aircraft lift aft. It was originally classed as the CVHA-1, and later as LPH-6. The *Thetis Bay* acted as an excellent test bed for helicopter landing ships to come. *Author's collection*

occasions, the troops were lost due to enemy shore batteries or simply overcrowding. The philosophy of the warlord was simple: get more troops.

Eventually, ships with individual bunks, good food, and more than adequate medical facilities became the norm. The rationale was simple: a trained fighting marine or soldier is the asset that wins. Jeopardizing this asset is morally and militarily foolish, and no longer permitted. Misusing men who were expected to fight was foolish and could cost a victory.

It was not until World War II compelled the use of synchronized and well-planned amphibious assaults that this aspect of naval warfare really took on a life of its own. In fact, the island-hopping strategy used to move Allied forces from Australia and the United States was based on progressive amphibious landings on islands leading to the Japanese home islands. It was a very successful plan.

The origin of amphibious warfare had been far below the standards of World War II, and certainly further below that of the twenty-first century. Today, effective amphibious planning, equipment, and naval and marine units devoted to this aspect of naval warfare make the difference in winning or losing. The future of naval warfare is intertwined in the amphibious element of a nation's navy, and no longer is wholly dependent on battleship or raw aircraft carrier support.

The first purpose-built helicopter carrier built from the keel up. This is the USS *Guadalcanal* (LPH-7), launched on March 16, 1963. This vessel is 18,300 tons full load and 598 feet long with an eighty-four-foot extreme beam on the flight deck. The *Guadalcanal* and its six sisters carried up to twenty UH-34 Seahorses (and later more modern helos) plus a full marine battalion. Helicopter insertion of marines or commandos (Great Britain) revolutionized amphibious warfare. *U.S. Navy*

The MV-22 Osprey (a Marine Corps variant of the V-22) is a twin-engine aircraft that can take off with its engines and huge propellers in a vertical position. When airborne, the engines/propellers are tilted forward to a horizontal position allowing the aircraft to fly forward at a maximum speed of 275 knots. It can land by reversing the process and make a vertical descent. With only a .50-caliber ramp-mounted machine gun, this leaves the MV-22 potentially vulnerable and unprotected. The Osprey has had a difficult growth from design to reality (1989–2005). Two tragic accidents delayed the project until all of the bugs could be worked out. The U.S. Marine Corps is expected to purchase 360 of these aircraft.

MV-22 OSPREY
Built by Bell Helicopter Textron/Boeing Defense and Space Group
Country: United States
Powerplant: two T406 AD400 Allison turboshafts
Top speed: 275 knots
Range: 515 miles or 2,100 nautical miles empty
Crew: 3

The USS *Tarawa* (LHA-1) moored in San Diego at the naval tation in 2004. The *Tarawa*, lead ship of the new LHA, was one of four amphibious carriers that are 820 feet in length, displace 39,900 tons, and have a beam of 146 feet on the flight deck. These ships have a top speed of twenty-four knots and can carry up to thirty-five helicopters and V/STOL aircraft. *Author's collection*

Expeditionary strike groups (ESGs), like this one led by the USS *Boxer* (LHD-4), have a minimum of one big-deck amphibious carrier and two support ships (LSD and LPD). In the future, littoral combat ships will be added and possibly a nuclear-guided missile submarine (SSGN). Its lift helos will be replaced in the future by the MV-22 Osprey. For combat purposes at sea, H-60 Seahawk ASW helos are also included in the ESG. The ESG is a navy within a navy.

EXPEDITIONARY STRIKE GROUP

Strike and heavy support: improved *Ticonderoga*-class cruiser (CG), two *Arleigh Burke* DDGs, one or more fast frigates, and a fast nuclear-attack submarine (SSN)

Ground component: Marine Expeditionary Unit (MEU)—a reinforced infantry battalion, reinforced helicopter squadron, and combat service units; 2,200 marines.

Air component: Harrier jets, Cobra attack helos, Sea Stallion and Sea Knight lift helos

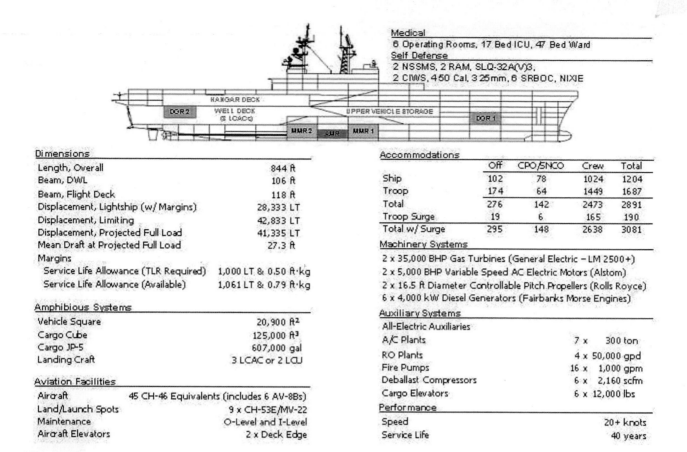

Medical
6 Operating Rooms, 17 Bed ICU, 47 Bed Ward
Self Defense
2 NSSMS, 2 RAM, SLQ-32A(V)3,
2 CIWS, 450 Cal, 3 25mm, 6 SRBOC, NIXIE

Dimensions	
Length, Overall	844 ft
Beam, DWL	106 ft
Beam, Flight Deck	118 ft
Displacement, Lightship (w/ Margins)	28,333 LT
Displacement, Limiting	42,833 LT
Displacement, Projected Full Load	41,335 LT
Mean Draft at Projected Full Load	27.3 ft
Margins	
Service Life Allowance (TLR Required)	1,000 LT & 0.50 ft·kg
Service Life Allowance (Available)	1,061 LT & 0.79 ft·kg

Amphibious Systems	
Vehicle Square	20,900 ft²
Cargo Cube	125,000 ft³
Cargo JP-5	607,000 gal
Landing Craft	3 LCAC or 2 LCU

Aviation Facilities	
Aircraft	45 CH-46 Equivalents (includes 6 AV-8Bs)
Land/Launch Spots	9 x CH-53E/MV-22
Maintenance	O-Level and I-Level
Aircraft Elevators	2 x Deck Edge

Accommodations	Off	CPO/SNCO	Crew	Total
Ship	102	78	1024	1204
Troop	174	64	1449	1687
Total	276	142	2473	2891
Troop Surge	19	6	165	190
Total w/ Surge	295	148	2638	3081

Machinery Systems
2 x 35,000 BHP Gas Turbines (General Electric – LM 2500+)
2 x 5,000 BHP Variable Speed AC Electric Motors (Alstom)
2 x 16.5 ft Diameter Controllable Pitch Propellers (Rolls Royce)
6 x 4,000 kW Diesel Generators (Fairbanks Morse Engines)

Auxiliary Systems		
All-Electric Auxiliaries		
A/C Plants	7 x	300 ton
RO Plants	4 x	50,000 gpd
Fire Pumps	16 x	1,000 gpm
Deballast Compressors	6 x	2,160 scfm
Cargo Elevators	6 x	12,000 lbs

Performance	
Speed	20+ knots
Service Life	40 years

Spec Sheet for the USS *Makin Island* (LHD-8), the most modern large-deck amphibious craft in the world. *U.S. Navy*

As of late 2006, the most modern and capable large-deck amphibious carrier: the USS *Makin Island* (LHD-8). The *Makin Island* is 844 feet in length; displaces 41,335 tons full load, and has a beam of 118 feet on the flight deck. This LHD carries up to forty-five CH-46 helos (including six AV-8B Harrier II fixed-wing jets) and/or other aircraft such as the Osprey. *U.S. Navy*

The HSV-X1 (the *Joint Venture* is shown here) is the most revolutionary transport craft yet acquired in the amphibious community. Currently, the U.S. military leases four of these high-speed wave-piercing craft from Australian companies. Along with *Joint Venture*, the *Swift, Spearhead,* and *Westpac Express* have been in constant use since becoming part of the amphibious picture, and a decision has been reached to outright purchase eight craft by 2011.

HSV-X1
Built on catamaran hulls and offered by Incat and Austral
Full-load displacement: 1,872 tons
Length: 318 feet; Beam: 88 feet
Propulsion: four caterpillar marine diesels
Top speed: 48 knots, light ship; 38 knots, fully loaded
Armament: small arms as yet
Aircraft capacity: two H-60 Seahawk helos

The USS *Pearl Harbor* (LSD-52) moored at the San Diego Naval Shipyard in 2005. The *Pearl Harbor* is the final ship of the *Whidbey Island* class of dock-landing ships begun in 1985. They are 609 feet in length and displace 15,939 tons full load. Their well deck is cavernous enough to handle two LCACs and the flight deck can accommodate at least two major helicopters or vertical takeoff fixed-wing aircraft. In concert with the big-deck amphibious craft, they are a perfect adjunct to the expeditionary strike group (ESG). *Author's collection*

Here is an idealized painting of the *San Antonio*–class transport dock ship USS *New York* (LPD-21) in New York harbor with the rebuilt World Trade Center featured. The real LPD has ten tons of steel from the destroyer structure melted into its construction. The *New York* should enter fleet service in two to three years and contribute to the decommissioning of at least four current amphibious ship classes.

SAN ANTONIO CLASS

Built by Northrop Grumman Ship Systems in the United States
Full-load displacement: 25,000 tons
Length: 684 feet; Beam: 105 feet
Propulsion: four sequentially turbocharged marine diesel engines generating 41,600 brake horsepower
Top speed: 22-plus knots
Armament: two Mark 31 Model 1 RAM launchers; two Mark 46 Model 1 30mm guns (stabilized mountings), and four 50-caliber MGs
Aircraft capacity: four of any combination of helo or MV 22 Osprey Tiltrotor
Capable of carrying 699 troops with fixed accommodations, and an additional 101 for a surge need

Here is a look at the USS *Pearl Harbor* (LSD-52)'s aft section and well deck door. Aside from being highly capable landing ships, they are heavily armed defensively. They are armed with two twenty-one-missile RAMs (RIM-116 missiles); two 20mm Phalanx Gatling guns (CIWS), and two single-barrel 25mm/.75-caliber Mark 38 Mod 0 Bushmasters. Aside from this close-in firepower, these LSDs are also armed with eight 12.7mm machine guns sited all over the ship to defeat suicide swimmers, boats, and close-in threats. *Author's collection*

A single-barrel 25mm Bushmaster aboard the USS *Tortuga* (LSD-46) of the *Whidbey Island* class. This weapon fires up to 250 high-explosive 25mm shells per minute, and has become modified to improve its accuracy and stability. *U.S. Navy*

USS *Germantown* (ISD-42) belongs to the twelve-unit *Whidbey Island* class of dock-landing ships. This class was built by Avondale Shipyards and Lockheed Shipbuilding in the United States.

WHIDBEY ISLAND CLASS
Built by Avondale Shipyards and Lockheed Shipbuilding in the United States
Commissioned: February 8, 1986
Full-load displacement: 15,939 tons
Length: 609 feet; Beam 84 feet
Propulsion: four medium speed/power diesel engines; 33,000 shaft horsepower
Armament: two RAM launchers; two 20mm Phalanx CIWS; two 25mm Mk 38 guns and six .50-caliber machine guns
Aircraft capacity: equivalent of two Super Stallion helos for vertical takeoff
Crew: 413 ship's company and 402 troops

A U.S. Marine Corps assault amphibious vehicle (AAV) has just emerged from the well deck of an amphibious attack warship. Its fundamental purpose is to get men from ship to shore. The edge of the well deck door can be seen underneath the AAV. Nearly seven hundred of the AAV family of 1,057 units are being upgraded with improved propulsion and weapons. The basic AAV weighs thirty-seven tons, can accommodate eighteen troops, and makes forty-five miles per hour on land. *U.S. Navy*

Republic of Korea (ROK) Marines, Naval Forces, and U.S. Marines cross the Yam Ha River during a realistic assault with explosions, smoke, and other difficulties certain to be encountered in a ship-to-shore attack. At least six AAVs can be seen making their way across the river. *U.S. Navy*

USS *Kearsarge* (LHD-3) prepares to accept an landing craft air cushion (LCAC) through its stern gate. The *Kearsarge* is a *Wasp*-class helicopter dock-landing ship or a "big-deck" amphibious carrier. *U.S. Navy*

WASP CLASS
Built by Ingalls Shipbuilding in the United States
Commissioned: September 25, 1993
Full-load displacement: 41,133 tons
Length: 844 feet; Beam: 140 feet
Propulsion: two boilers, two gas turbines; 70,000 shaft horsepower
Top speed: 20-plus knots
Armament: two RAM launchers, two NATO Sea Sparrow launchers, three CIWS 20mm Phalanx guns, four .50-caliber MGs, and four Mk 38 25mm MGs
Aircraft capacity: a mix of AV-3B Harriers, MV-22 Ospreys, and various helos up to forty-six aircraft.
Crew: 1,108; can carry up to 2,000 equipped marines

HMS *Bulwark* L-15 of the Royal Navy's *Albion* class of LPD or amphibious transport dock. The *Bulwark* entered service in December 2004, and has been active in Task Force 150 off the East African coast searching for pirates. This ship and its sisters displace 16,981 tons full load and carry up to 710 troops in a surge attack mode. The air group consists of three *Sea King* helicopters. *U.S. Navy*

The Italian MM *San Giorgio* (L9892) class of which there are three ships. This class can carry five Sea King or AB-212 helicopters on deck and three LCMs or MTMs in a floodable deck. In addition, the ship has the capability of launching and recovering three LCVPs using thirty-ton-capacity lifts (davits) on a portside sponson. *U.S. Navy*

The Japanese Maritime Self Defense Force (JMSDF) has built the *Osumi*-class LST. It looks like an aircraft carrier—a direct violation of their constitution. The flight deck will handle two Chinook helos. There are three ships in this class, and the JMSDF is also building a DDH that is a combination of a powerful destroyer and an aircraft carrier. *U.S. Navy*

Two up-to-date LSTs at the Royal Thailand Amphibious Base near Bangkok in July 2006: HTMS *Sichang* (LST-721) and HTMS *Surin* (722). The PS-700 class was built indigenously in Bangkok in the late 1980s, and the 4,235-ton, 337-foot-long craft can make up to sixteen knots. They are helicopter capable; the crew can beach the ship in less than nine feet of water. *Author's collection*

South Korean LP-X *Dokdo* (LP-X, or landing platform experimental) amphibious ship, which is a direct response to the Japanese *Osumi* class. The LP-X, however, is 655 feet in length, 105 feet wide, and displaces eighteen thousand tons. Its four diesels drive it at twenty-two knots maximum, and it is capable of carrying up to fifteen rotary wing or VTOL aircraft. This could include EH-101 Merlin helos, and a well deck aft that will house two LCACs or like vessels. *U.S. Navy*

A utility landing craft (LCU) fully loaded with eleven Hummers from the marines of the 26th Marine Expeditionary Unit (MEU) for transport from the USS *Shreveport* (LPD-12). LCU-1645 is one of seventy-one craft built that are self-propelled by four diesel engines. The LCU is 437 tons full load and is capable of eleven knots with light armament for defense. The crew of twelve includes two officers. The LCU or conventional landing craft is being phased out in favor of the LCAC and other, more modern amphibians. *U.S. Navy*

The well deck of the USS *Harpers Ferry* (LSD-49), an amphibious attack ship is filled with assault amphibians (AAV) of the 31st Marine Expeditionary Unit awaiting their time to move out. They will exit through the aft well deck gate for their practice operation in the Yellow Sea. This rehearsal is necessary to hone the skills of the crews and marines who will ride back and forth (almost submerged). *U.S. Navy*

The LCAC class is an inventive and highly utilitarian landing craft that does not stop at the high-water mark. Because it is driven by gas turbine propellers, the craft is much like a swamp runner and can maneuver on water, mud, sand, and dirt. This eliminates the need for dirt causeways from landing ships to get troops and equipment ashore, and can take marines to the battle site much quicker. Pictured is the LCAC 41. Ninety-one total LCACs are in the U.S. Navy inventory. *U.S. Navy*

LCAC CLASS
Built by Textron in New Orleans
Commissioned: November 27, 1991
Full-load displacement: 166.6 tons
Length: 88 feet; Beam: 47 feet
Propulsion: four AVCO TF40B gas turbines: two used for lift, two for movement
Top speed: 54 knots, 40 knots when fully loaded
Armament: none except small arms
Load carried: five crew and 180 troops when fitted for personnel only; cargo and vehicles: sixty tons, seventy-five tons overload

The Westland Lynx helicopter, which is in use throughout the world. The Lynx is about to land on the USS *Saipan* (LHA-2). The helo carries a crew of three and can carry troops and weapons such as torpedoes, Sea Skua missiles, and machine guns. It has a range of 328 miles and a cruising speed of 158 miles per hour. *U.S. Navy*

An AH-1 Cobra. This is an attack helicopter that provides ground support and air support to other helos as necessary. It has a maximum speed of 190 knots and a range of 256 miles. The Cobra is armed with a 20mm cannon, TOW, Hellfire Sidearm, and Sidewinder missiles. The Cobra can also carry 2.75- or five-inch rockets in pods. *U.S. Navy*

Shown is a marine Sea Knight being loaded with humanitarian supplies for those in need ashore. The Sea Knight is a general-transport helicopter capable of a moderate load of people, equipment, and supplies. It has served the U.S. Navy and the Marine Corps since 1962.
U.S. Navy

CH-46 SEA KNIGHT
Built by the Boeing Company, Vertol
    Division, United States
Powerplant: two GE turboshafts; 3,740 hp
Top speed: 143 knots
Armament: none
Range: 540 nautical miles (mission)
Crew: 2
Note: The 44-year-old basic Sea Knight is
    being slowly retired and replaced by
    more modern rotary wing aircraft.

The ever-dependable HH-60-series Seahawk can elude enemy missiles by dropping flares (heat interception threats) and chaff (radar-guided missiles). This Seahawk is tasked with antisubmarine work, and is assigned to the USS *Essex* (LHD-2) Expeditionary Group operating in the Northern Persian Gulf (December 21, 2004). *U.S. Navy*

A U.S. Marine Corps CH-53 Super Stallion takes off from the USS *Peleliu* (LHA-5). The CH-53 is a huge aircraft and weighs 73,500 pounds fully loaded. With its powerful three engines, it can fly at a maximum of 170 knots with a range of 580 nautical miles. Aside from seating fifty-five passengers, the Super Stallion can lift a humvee, a 155mm howitzer, or a light armored vehicle. In short, this aircraft can transport heavy equipment right to the battlefield. *U.S. Navy*

An AV-8B Harrier II begins a slow takeoff from a big-deck amphibious carrier. This Harrier is a direct descendent of the Sea Harrier that performed so well for the British in the 1982 Falklands War. The upgraded models have a top speed of 675 miles per hour with a range of 1,200 nautical miles. They are armed with 25mm cannons and have seven pylons for various missiles and bombs of all types. *U.S. Navy*

CRUISERS AND DESTROYERS

Cruisers and Destroyers

From the beginning of the twentieth century and up through 1941, the battleship reigned supreme as the capital ship of any nation seeking a power seat at the international table of nations. Proud lines of huge grey ships paraded in and out of harbors and gave comfort to nations that—without question—believed in their absolute invincibility. Unfortunately, the Achilles' heel of the battleship consisted of a lightweight, inexpensive aircraft carrying a bomb or torpedo. Few believed this was possible, and those who should have known better laughed at the idea.

Soon, the myth of the unprotected battleship against air attack was proven on three very graphic occasions. First, the November 11, 1940, Royal Navy aircraft carrier attack on the Italian fleet based at Taranto that destroyed their surface ship threat in the region was followed up by the December 7, 1941, Japanese attack on Pearl Harbor. This attack rendered six battleships (old) forever destroyed or damaged. Three days after the air attack on Pearl Harbor, the Japanese located *Force Z* near Singapore and sank the Royal Navy's HMS *Prince of Wales* and HMS *Repulse* on December 10, 1941. All of the attacks were highly successful by aircraft either from ground bases or aircraft carriers. Within the period of thirteen months, it became obvious that the aircraft carrier had supplanted the battleship as the capital ship. During the latter years of World War II, battleships such as the *Iowa* and *South Dakota* classes were very heavily armed with defensive antiaircraft weaponry (120 weapons), and made excellent escorts for the fast carriers. As the war ended, however, and the brushfire wars with Soviet-backed nations began, the aircraft carrier now reigned supreme.

Previous page: An *Iowa*-class battleship lets loose with its main battery and shoots to port and starboard. The navies of the world can no longer afford such large labor-intensive ships for gunfire support. *U.S. Navy*

The battleship USS *New Jersey* (BB-62) leads a column of surface ships in the late 1980s. The USS *Iowa* (BB-61) follows and next is the nuclear-powered cruiser USS *Long Beach* (CGN-9). All have been stricken from the U.S. Navy and replaced by digital-systems warships. Despite having little value in today's ocean warfare, these ships were aesthetically beautiful in their day. *U.S. Navy*

Peru's light cruiser *Almirante Grau* (CLM-81) fires its forward Bofors six-inch guns in 2006. Armed with eight Otomat Mk 2 surface-to-surface missiles, its main battery is four twin-barrel 152mm/.52-caliber dual-purpose guns. The 616-foot, 12,165-ton ship is capable of thirty-two knots, and is the last gun cruiser in the world. *U.S. Navy*

Surface ships, however, still had great value to the fleets of the world, and as the twentieth century came and went, the cruiser and destroyer slowly became the new capital ships of the surface fleet. The destroyer type was needed to check the Soviet submarine force after World War II, and the cruiser was used for gunfire support and antiaircraft escort with a new weapon: the guided missile.

The American cruiser has also taken the first steps in antiballistic missile defense—crucial to survival in a nuclear age when rogue nations now possess the ability to launch crude but deadly missiles laden with nuclear weapons. This was never dreamed of even a quarter century ago, and now is becoming a truism for the world's navies as well as the U.S. Navy.

Superpowers arose out of the embers of World War II. The Soviet and Warsaw Pact nations in concert with the People's Liberation Army (Navy) (PLAN) and other Southeast Asian Communist states had to build new navies, as relatively small navies had been destroyed during the war. The Soviet Union slowly embarked on a building program beginning with cruisers, nuclear submarines, missile cruisers, and destroyers, and armed its surface ships with antiship and antiair missiles as their main battery. Conversely, the U.S. Navy had to be content with retrofitting its chronologically new, but technologically obsolescing warships—the World War II inventory. It was not until the mid 1970s that the U.S. Navy and other Western navies began to build up-to-date—from the keel up—missile destroyers and cruisers.

Overall, detection and weaponry have become increasingly sophisticated over the last few decades, and the ships themselves can now almost compete with today's submarines on a level playing field. Yet, the superquiet diesel-electric boats are again posing a serious challenge to Western navies. The solution to this problem is currently under study, and must be resolved quickly. If not, then the diesel-electric submarine will be the winner in any contest within littoral waters. In addition, smaller vessels are becoming popular as firepower increases without the commensurate size of the vessel. This will be the future of naval forces afloat.

The U.S. Navy's missile cruiser USS *Philippine Sea* (CG-58) is one of the original twenty-seven *Ticonderoga*-class *Aegis*/missile cruisers built from 1983 to 1994. They were expensive and revolutionary vessels designed to defeat Soviet Bear and Badger bombers as well as swarm antiship missile attacks. The cruisers were initially considered gold plated; however, their capabilities more than justified the costs when they were employed in various brushfire wars. From this class, the *Arleigh Burke*–class destroyer was born with the *Aegis* system of acquire, track, designate, and determine a course of action against airborne or ocean-going threat. The original five (CG-47 through CG-51) have been surplused. The remaining twenty-two CGs (improved *Ticonderoga*) will be upgraded to increase their life by five to ten additional years (total forty years). *U.S. Navy*

TICONDEROGA CLASS
Full-load displacement: in excess of 10,000 tons
Propulsion: gas turbine engines; 100,000 shaft horsepower
Top speed: 30-plus knots
Armament: two Mk 41 VLS missile launchers (122 silos or cells) firing a variety of
    missiles, two single 5-inch Mk 45 automatic guns, Phalanx 20mm CIWS
Aircraft capacity: two SH-60B Seahawk Lamps III

The American *Ticonderoga*-class (improved) cruiser USS *Vella Gulf* (CG-72) dwarfs the 248-ton full-load Finnish *Rauma (Helsinki II* class) while on maneuvers. The *Vella Gulf* is one of the original twenty-seven *Ticonderoga*-class *Aegis*-class cruisers in the U.S. Navy, and now with the decommissioning of the first five cruisers in the class (CG-47–51), there are twenty-two improved *Ticonderoga*–class cruisers. The *Vella Gulf* displaces more than ten thousand tons and is 566 feet in length. *U.S. Navy*

Three U.S. *Arleigh Burke* destroyers flying Old Glory pass in review. From top to bottom are the USS *Shoup* (DDG-86), USS *Lassen* (DDG-82), and the USS *McCampbell* (DDG-85). These are the most modern destroyers in the world. *U.S. Navy*

The USS *Russell* (DDG-59), an *Arleigh Burke*–class *Aegis*/missile destroyer, is equipped with the latest in systems designed to detect, designate, track, and prioritize weapons for an appropriate response. The *Russell* is paying its respects at the sixty-fifth anniversary of the Japanese attack on Pearl Harbor at exactly 0755 on December 7, 2006. *Author's collection*

USS *RUSSELL*
Built by Ingalls Ship Systems, Mississippi
Commissioned: May 20, 1995
Full-load displacement: 8,850 tons
Propulsion: four GE gas turbine engines generating up to 105,000 shaft horsepower
Top speed: 31-plus knots
Armament: two VLS launchers; total of 96 cells or silos for a variety of missiles (ASROC, standard, and Tomahawk), a single 127mm/.54-caliber gun forward (5 inches), Phalanx 20mm CIWS, ASW torpedo tubes for Mk 46, Mk 50 torpe does, and smaller weapons such as the 25mm Bushmaster MG
Aircraft capacity: two SH-60R Seahawk helicopters

Four *Aegis* warships (cruisers and destroyers) fire a coordinated volley of missiles from their vertical launch systems (VLS). In the far distance are the cruiser USS *Vicksburg* (CG-59), then the destroyers USS *Roosevelt* (DDG-80), USS *Carney* (DDG-64), and USS *The Sullivans* (DDG-68). This image is dated December 2003. *U.S. Navy*

The brain of the *Aegis* system in an *Arleigh Burke* destroyer. The SPY-1A or -1B radar system is a phased array that can sweep 360 degrees; tied to this is a system that can identify, track, prioritize, and select appropriate weapons to defeat any threat based on predetermined criteria. It is truly an amazing system that is capable of allowing a single warship to fight off multiple threats— automatically. *U.S. Navy*

Japan's JMSDF *Kongo* (DDG-173) operates in a combined task force with U.S. Navy ships. The *Kongo* class currently has four ships and is *Aegis*/missile equipped. There is an upgraded series of *Aegis* warships being built (DDG-177 and DDG-178). *U.S. Navy*

KONGO CLASS
Built by Mitsubishi—Tokyo
Full-load displacement: 9,485 tons
Propulsion: GE gas turbines; 100,000 shaft horsepower
Top speed: 30 knots
Armament: a single 5-inch/.62-caliber gun, harpoon missiles, two 20mm Phalanx CIWS and 90 cells in the VLS launch system; triple ASW tubes for Mk 46 and Mk 50 torpedoes
Aircraft capacity: temporary landing/takeoff platform for helo

The forward 127mm/.54-caliber Mark 45 gun aboard the USS *Barry* (DDG-52) fires at a target. Ships in this class with a number higher than DDG-80 now have the 127mm/.62-caliber gun plus other improved weapons systems. *U.S. Navy*

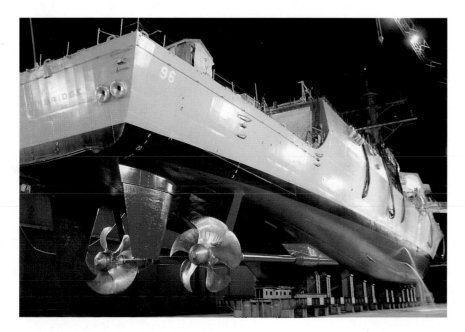

The USS *Bainbridge* (DDG-96) out of water at the builder's yard at Bath Iron Works in Bath, Maine. Note the highly polished five-blade props that contribute to this destroyer's more than thirty knots speed. *U.S. Navy*

The former Soviet (now Russian) *Sovremennyy* (DDG, or guided missile destroyer). These are powerful and well-equipped destroyers, and the PLAN now has two that were transferred in the early twenty-first century. Two more are to be transferred to Mainland China by 2010; however, the retro-fitted *Kidd* class is far more capable as a war-fighter than the *Sovremennyy* class. *Author's collection*

The ex-USS *Callaghan* (DDG-994), one of four *Kidd*-class destroyers built for the Shah of Iran but kept by the U.S. Navy. The *Kidd* class was primarily designed for concentrated antiair defense. All have been refurbished and sold to Taiwan. These four destroyers are more than an even match for any destroyer in the PLAN's inventory. The acquisition of the four *Kidd*s restored the balance of naval power between the People's Republic and the PLAN. *Author's collection*

The Royal Danish Navy's *Peter Skram* (F-352), a 2,700-ton full-load destroyer of 1960s vintage. It has been armed with a Sea Sparrow launcher, five-inch guns (American twin-mount design), and Harpoon antiship missiles (forward and in the number 2 gun mount position). As of 2003, it was permanently moored at the Copenhagen Navy Yard (with the Royal Danish family's yacht). *Author's collection*

The Russian destroyer *Nastoychivvy* (meaning "persistent") is part of the *Sovremennyy* class in the Baltic Fleet. It is one of ten in this class that are powerful and menacing, yet not a match for an *Arleigh Burke* destroyer or even a 1980s *Kidd* class. Two have been transferred to the Chinese PLA (N) to equalize the destroyer forces between Taiwan and mainland China—hence the transfer of four *Kidd*-class DDGs to Taiwan by the United States. *U.S. Navy*

SOVREMENNYY CLASS
Built by Severnaya Yard, St. Petersburg, Russia; 1986–1994
Commissioned: March 27, 1993
Full-load displacement: 8,480 tons
Length: 156 meters
Armament: Sunburn missiles (SSM) SA-N-7 SAM battery, two twin 130mm/.54-caliber guns, four single 30mm/.54-caliber MGs, and various ASW torpe does and rockets
Aircraft capacity: single Ka-27PL Helix helicopter or a Ka-27RT targeting helo

The fast frigate USS *Paul* (FF-1080) in rough seas. The *Paul* was one of the large class of frigates built to protect convoys on their way to NATO nations in the event of a conventional war with the Soviet Union. The *Knox* class displaced 4,200 tons (full load) and were 438 feet in length. They were generally armed with a LAMPS helicopter for ASW, a five-inch/.54-caliber gun, Sea Sparrow launcher and missiles, four fixed torpedoes, and a single 20mm Phalanx CIWS. The *Knox*es could make twenty-seven knots on a steam turbine powerplant. None of these ships are active U.S. Navy assets, yet many have been sold or transferred to other nations. *Author's collection*

Russian–guided-missile destroyer *Marshal Shaposhnikov* enters Agana Harbor in Guam. The *Udaloy* class displaces 8,404 tons full load and is 536 feet in length. It is armed with SS-N-14 ASW/antiship SSM, a 100mm/.70-caliber DP gun, two Helix ASW helicopters, and close-in weapons. *U.S. Navy*

The USS *Rueben James* (FFG-57) in Hong Kong harbor, August 2006. It is a unit in the U.S. Navy's *Oliver Hazard Perry* fast frigate class (1979–1989). At one time, the U.S. Navy had more than one hundred frigates or ocean-escort vessels during the Cold War with the Soviet bloc nations. *Author's collection*

USS *RUEBEN JAMES*
Built by Todd Shipyards, San Pedro,
    California
Commissioned: March 22, 1986
Full-load displacement: 4,108 tons
Length: 455 feet
Propulsion: two GE gas turbine engines;
    41,000 shaft horsepower
Top speed: 29 knots
Armament: one 76mm/.62-caliber Mk 75 DP
    gun, Phalanx 20mm CIWS, two triple-
    tube ASW torpedo tubes for Mk 46 or
    Mk 50 torpedoes
Aircraft capacity: one or two SH-60B
    Seahawk Lamps helo

A Royal Australian Navy frigate of the *ANZAC* class fires its forward 127mm/.54-caliber gun. The *ANZAC* class is relatively new and displaces 3,600 tons (full load) with a maximum speed of twenty-seven knots. They are heavily armed frigates, and carry a Super Seasprite helicopter aft. *Author's collection*

HMAS *Sydney* (FFG-03) operates in the North Arabian Gulf near offshore oil platforms. Its task is to protect these assets from hit-and-run insurgents or small fast-attack craft from Iran. The *Sydney* was built to U.S. Navy standards and is generally a replica of the *Oliver Hazard Perry* class. *Author's collection*

The United Kingdom's fast frigate HMS *Richmond* (F-239) fires a AGM-84A Harpoon at the target ship ex-USS *Wainwright* (older missile cruiser). The *Richmond* is one of the sixteen *Duke*-class frigates at 4,300 tons full load. This frigate is capable of twenty-eight knots and has the entire array of weapons, including a Merlin HM Mk 1 helicopter. *U.S. Navy*

A "pepperbox" ASROC launcher from the early 1960s. The box launcher was a common method of deploying the ASROC missile with the homing torpedo warhead. Most destroyers, frigates, and some cruisers had eight missiles in the box. Later, the pepperbox was eliminated in favor of today's vertical launch system. *Author's collection*

A twenty-kiloton warhead on a homing torpedo detonates after being launched on an ASROC missile from the destroyer USS *Ager-holm* (DD-826). The test was successful, but never repeated because the hulls of most destroyers and ASW ships could not withstand the vibration of a submerged nuclear blast. A nuclear test ban treaty also intervened and put an end to this type of weaponry. *U.S. Navy*

A triple-tube Mark 32 ASW torpedo launcher for Mk 46 and Mk 50 lightweight torpedoes (8.5 feet long and 509 pounds in overall weight). The torpedoes have a variety of warheads and the most common is the 99.86-pound HE. The torpedoes can dive to six hundred meters or 1,968 feet at a speed of forty knots. The USS *Preble* (DDG-88) has just fired a Mk 46 torpedo, and it is one of fourteen thousand in the U.S. Navy's inventory. *U.S. Navy*

The Spanish *Aegis*-equipped frigate, *Alvaro de Bazan* (F-101) about to recover its AWS helicopter, a SH-60B Seahawk. The ASW helicopter coupled with a powerful and well-armed warship is a lethal threat to any submarine. Spain is among a very few nations that have access to the hardware and software that make up the *Aegis* system. The *Bazan* is able to make 28.5 knots on a CODOG propulsion system of gas turbine and diesel power. It is armed with a forty-eight-cell VLS containing a variety of contemporary missiles in addition to its CIWS gun and a five-inch/.54-caliber gun forward. *Author's collection*

The *Surcouf* (F-711) fast frigate (French Republic, *La Fayette* class) comes alongside the USS *Seattle* for replenishment in this 2002 image. *U.S. Navy*

SURCOUF FAST FRIGATE
Built by DCN, Lorient, France
Commissioned: February 7, 1997
Full-load displacement: 3,600 tons
Propulsion: turbocharged diesel engines;
    21,000 brake horsepower
Top speed: 25 knots
Armament: Exocet SSM, Crotale SAM,
    100mm/.55-caliber gun forward and two
    single 20mm/.90-caliber MGs
Aircraft capacity: one Panther helicopter

The Indonesian fast frigate *Karel Satuitubun*, which is one of six ex-Netherlands *Van Speijk*–class ships transferred to Indonesia in the 1980s. This class was built during the 1960s for the Netherlands and is roughly similar to the Royal Navy's highly successful *Leander* class. They are 2,940 tons full load and carry the typical retrofitted weapons of the late twentieth century. *U.S. Navy*

A Chinese (PLAN) destroyer of the *Luhai* (Project 52) class. This is the *Shenzhen*, which entered service in January 1999. This vessel is capable of twenty-nine knots on two gas-turbine engines connected to two turbo diesels. This class is armed with SSM and SAM missiles in concert with ASW torpedoes and a twin 100mm/.55-caliber gun mount. There are also four twin 37mm guns for close-in defense, and a Ka-28 Helix A helicopter for ASW and other tasks. *U.S. Navy*

The *Hamburg* is a German *Sachsen*-class (type 124) frigate with an armament that includes harpoon antiship missiles, a thirty-two-cell VLS launcher for standard missiles and evolved Sea Sparrow SAM, a 76mm/.62-caliber OTO Melara gun forward, two RAM 21 missile systems and triple ASW torpedo tubes. Here are three ships in the *Sachsen* class that all have a phased array system similar to the U.S. Navy's *Aegis* Spy-1D. *U.S. Navy*

HAMBURG **FRIGATE**
Built by HDW, Kiel, Germany
Commissioned: December 15, 2004
Propulsion: CODAG—diesel and gas turbine;
     51,600 horsepower
Top speed: 29 knots
Aircraft capacity: two Super Lynx helos

The German *Lubeck* (F-214) participating in a NATO operation. The *Lubeck* is one of eight *Bremen*-class (type 122A) 3,800-ton f/l frigates built during the 1980s. The *Bremen*s are armed with Sea Sparrow missiles, two RAM launchers with twenty-one missiles, eight Harpoon anti-ship missiles, and one 76mm/.62-caliber OTO Melara gun. In addition, the close-in weapon consists of two single 20mm/.90-caliber weapons, and the ASW is adequately covered by two fixed twin 324mm ASW torpedo tubes and two Lynx Mk 88 helicopters. *U.S. Navy*

The Kingdom of the Netherlands *Tromp* (F-803) maneuvers into its berth at the Pearl Harbor Naval Station on November 10, 2006, in order to be a part of the sixty-fifth anniversary of the attack on Pearl Harbor by the Japanese Navy and naval air forces. *U.S. Navy*

The Canadian fast frigate HMCS *Toronto* is one of twelve ships in the *Halifax* class. It has an armament that includes a harpoon SSM, VLS for Sea Sparrow SAM, 57mm/.70-caliber Bofors and Phalanx Gatling CIWS, and ASW torpedoes (Mk 46 and Mk 50) for triple-tube mounting. *U.S. Navy*

HALIFAX CLASS
Built by St. John Shipbuilding, New Brunswick
Commissioned: July 29, 1993
Full-load displacement: 4,761 tons
Length: 445 feet
Propulsion: two GE gas turbine engines and diesels; 47,494 shaft horsepower
Aircraft capacity: one CH-124A Sea King helo

A bow on view of the Ecuadorian corvette *BAE El Oro* (CM-14). This is one of six of the Italian-built *Wadi M'ragh* class, and is hunting for a suspected drug-running tramp freighter off the coast. These seven-hundred-ton full-load combatants or Guided Missile Patrol boats are capable of thirty-seven knots and carry a 6mm 40 Exocet SSM and a 76mm/.62-caliber OTO Melara gun forward and a twin 40mm/.70-caliber OTO Melara AA mount aft. In addition, this class also has facilities for a Bell 206B helicopter. *U.S. Navy*

SUBMARINES

Submarines

The first military submarine was the seventeenth-century Ukrainian *chaika*, which was simply used for reconnaissance and infiltration missions. The first well-known and powered attack submarine was the famous American Colonial boat dubbed the *Turtle*. It was a wooden barrel-like affair powered by the operator turning a screw and ultimately ramming a mine, torpedo, or bomb into the hull of a British ship of the line.

For the first four decades of the twentieth century, the submarine basically remained a military tool. World War I and World War II saw the submarine rise from coastal scouting roles to one of the most potent weapons of war ever designed. The hull structure emerged from carbon steel to alloyed steel or titanium and continues in this fashion into the twenty-first century.

During both World Wars, the submarine was dedicated to the destruction of the enemy's communication and supply lines. By the end of World War II, the Allied submarine forces literally destroyed the Japanese Empire and starved its population by sinking interisland freighters and destroying supply runs to island posts in the Pacific.

By 1955, Americans had harnessed nuclear power in a submersible, the USS *Nautilus* (SSN-571), and from that point the wealthier Western nations and the Soviet Union began building nuclear-powered attack (SSN), guided missile (SSGN), and intercontinental ballistic missile (SSBN) submarines as quickly as budgets would allow.

Great strides were made in nuclear power, although the problem of noise due to the

Previous page: The USS *Tang* (SS-563) leaves Pearl Harbor on a patrol during the mid 1960s. The *Tang* was a diesel-electric-powered boat that could sail at twenty knots on the surface and for short periods; twenty-seven knots submerged. The 2,260-ton displacement *Tang* was turned over to Iran with the USS *Wahoo* and USS *Trout*. Before the *Trout* was taken from New London in December 1979, the Iranian crew abandoned and fled. The *Tang* is an excellent diesel-electric submarine representative in the immediate postwar period. *U.S. Navy*

steam powerplant was difficult to remedy. The diesel-electric boat (SS) was still quieter and could operate more effectively in the coastal or littoral waters. Many nations began to optimize the diesel power system and at the same time studied other methods of propulsion, remaining underwater for ten to fourteen days.

The U.S. Navy once managed to have dozens of nuclear attack and ballistic missile submarines roaming the world's oceans. The target was simple: the Soviet Navy and, in particular, any of its undersea branches with emphasis on the ballistic missile. The Western navies planned to destroy as many intercontinental ballistic missiles (ICBMs) or "boomers" as possible prior to them being launched at Western civilian and military targets. Also targeted were the SSGN classes of cruise missile boats such as the *Juliett*, *Echo*, *Charlie*, and *Yankee* classes.

Likewise, the Soviet Navy followed the same doctrine: destroy the American *George Washington*, *Lafayette*, *Ethan Allen*, *Ohio*, and other U.S. Navy ICBM launch platforms before they could send their missiles against Kiev, Moscow, Leningrad, etc. When the Soviet Union imploded economically, socially, and militarily, there was little use for scores of nuclear attack and missile submarines on either side. The majority of the Soviet Union's nuclear submarines began to rot in the backwaters of out-of-the-way naval bases and abandoned harbors.

As to the West, there are less than two dozen boomers, and approximately ninety nuclear attack craft. The eighteen-boat *Ohio* class, which has a displacement of 18,750 tons submerged, is now fourteen strong and the other four have been converted to guided missile boats (SSGN) that carry 154 Tomahawk cruise missiles and a provision for insertion/extraction of special operations forces.

Many nations are now quite interested in nonnuclear forms of propulsion due to costs and far quieter operations. The most promising is the air independent fuel cell system aboard the German Type 21/Type 214 models of attack submarine. These models have been under development, and orders have been placed for a number of units.

When a truly adept method of operating a submersible for a near unlimited time underwater at near full power comes about, nuclear propulsion will be a powerplant of the past. Until such time, atomic power will be the best that designers can offer.

Two ancient Russian/Soviet diesel attack boats. At one time, the Soviet Union had the largest submarine force in the world; however, many were old-fashioned, poorly built deathtraps. To the right is a modified *Romeo* class. On the left, a *Whiskey* class. There were 236 boats in the *Whiskey* class built for the defense of the motherland, and eventually many were sold off. *Author's collection*

Japan's JMSDF *Oyashio* (SS-590) is part of a ten-boat class with an armament of six 533mm bow torpedo tubes to accommodate harpoon and type HU-603B torpedoes. *U.S. Navy*

JMSDF *OYASHIO*
Built by Kawasaki, Kobe
Commissioned: March 16, 1998
Full-load displacement: 3,600 tons submerged
Length: 81.70 meters
Propulsion: two diesel engines and electric power for submerged operations
Top speed: 12 knots surface; 20 knots submerged
Crew: 10 officers, 59 enlisted

The USS *Virginia* (SSN-774) (built by General Dynamics Electric Boat Division) was delivered to the U.S. Navy on June 23, 2004, and is the first of thirty attack submarines in this class. The *Virginia*s are 7,800 tons full load and capable of thirty-five knots submerged. These boats carry thirty-eight weapons, including sixteen Tomahawk missiles and Mk 48 ADCAP torpedoes. *U.S. Navy*

The *Galerna* (S-71), a Spanish Navy diesel-electric boat built in Spain by Izar at Cartegena. It is a French *Agosta* (S-70) model that displaces 1,750 tons submerged and is capable of twelve knots surfaced and 20.5 knots submerged. There were four boats built to the French S-70 specifications during the late 1970s and mid 1980s. They are armed with four 550mm bow torpedo tubes and can fire torpedoes or launch up to nineteen mines. These are relatively modern conventional submarines and popular among many nations. *Author's collection*

The USS *Los Angeles* (SSN-688), the namesake and lead ship of a class of nuclear-attack submarines built in the United States beginning in 1976. Over a twenty-year period, sixty-two *Los Angeles*–class boats were commissioned. As of 2006, fifty remain, and twelve have been inactivated. This class set the stage for nuclear-attack submarines in the late twentieth century; however, the rapid decommissioning of these craft has placed an undue strain on the U.S. Navy's ability to maintain a credible attack submarine force. The inability to refuel without cutting up the boat ranks with keeping pre–World War I battleships beyond their usefulness. *U.S. Navy*

The USS *Dallas* (SSN-700) is one of the fifty *Los Angeles* class of boats in service. Initially, there were sixty-two vessels in the class. The *Dallas* is shown here with a dry-dock shelter and a swimmer delivery vehicle aboard. The swimmer delivery vehicle can insert SEALs in a target area and return them to the host submarine. Its armament includes four 533mm torpedo tubes amidships that can fire Tomahawk missiles and Mk 48/Mk 48 ADCAP torpedoes. *U.S. Navy*

USS *DALLAS*
Built by Electric Boat Company
Commissioned: July 18, 1981
The swimmer delivery vehicle was built by Stidd Systems and likely was launched in 2002.
Propulsion: nuclear power (GE S6G pressurized water reactor)
Full-load displacement: 6,977 tons submerged
Top speed: 30-plus knots submerged

The USS *North Carolina* (SSN-777) under construction by General Dynamics Electric Boat Division. Like the others in the class, the *North Carolina* is 7,800 tons full load and capable of thirty-five knots submerged. Its crew consists of twelve officers and 101 enlisted personnel.
U.S. Navy

A *Golf II* SSBN (intercontinental ballistic missile submarine) that sunk in the Pacific in 1968. The *Golf* SSBNs were crude, but contained data necessary to national defense during that time period. Later, an operation utilizing the 63,000-ton *Glomar Explorer* brought up a large portion of the boat for examination by U.S. Navy technicians.
Author's collection

USS *Texas* (SSN-775) is one of the newer *Virginia*-class nuclear-attack submarines. It is one of five currently in service or close to commissioning. The *Virginia* class is slated to have thirty boats that are far superior to the *Los Angeles* class (its predecessor). Its armament includes twelve vertical launch tubes for Tomahawk missiles, mines, and Mk 48 ADCAP torpedoes. The nuclear powerplant should last up to thirty years of full service, which is a vast improvement over the *Los Angeles* class.
U.S. Navy

USS *TEXAS*
Built by Newport News Shipyard
Commissioned: June 23, 2004
Full-load displacement: 7,800 tons
Top speed: 35 knots submerged
Propulsion: 40,000 shaft horsepower, single nuclear reactor

Like something out of a Las Vegas magic show, the USS *Jimmy Carter* (SSN-23) goes into a deperming facility or a magnetic silencing facility at the Bangor complex of the Kitsap Naval Base. This series of charged wires reduces the electromagnetic signature of this *Sea Wolf*-class submarine. This is one of the vital treatments to ensuring that an enemy with a high degree of technology cannot detect this boat. *U.S. Navy*

The *Yankee I* ballistic missile boat could launch sixteen missiles from inside their pressure hulls. The SS-N-6 or Serb missile had a range of 240 kilometers and was a one-megaton nuclear weapon. The *Yankee* closely resembled the Polaris boats fielded by the U.S. Navy. Most *Yankee*s patrolled the U.S. coasts and did not have to surface to fire their missiles. The captains made certain that their boats avoided Orion ASW aircraft patrols. *U.S. Navy*

YANKEE I BALLISTIC MISSILE BOAT
One of thirty-four SSBNs built in Leningrad, Soviet Union, from 1969 to 1972
Full-load displacement: 9,600 tons submerged
Top speed: 30 knots submerged
Propulsion: nuclear powerplant
Length: 427 feet

The U.S. Navy's cutaway of the new *Ohio*-class SSGN: Tomahawk missiles, swimmer lockouts, and SEAL dry-dock shelters for insertion and extraction. *U.S. Navy*

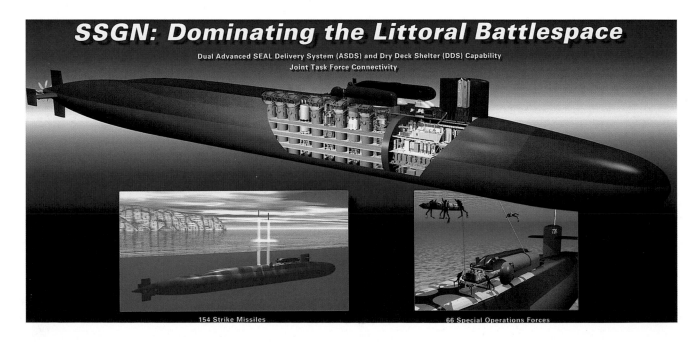

SSGN: Dominating the Littoral Battlespace
Dual Advanced SEAL Delivery System (ASDS) and Dry Deck Shelter (DDS) Capability
Joint Task Force Connectivity

154 Strike Missiles

66 Special Operations Forces

The USS *Ohio* (SSBN-726) enters a dry-dock at the Puget Sound Naval Shipyard for conversion to a guided missile/special operations boat. The *Ohio* and three of its sisters (*Michigan*, *Florida*, and *Georgia*) were to be converted to SSGNs that could fire up to 154 Tomahawk missiles and can carry squads of SEALs to areas where special forces are needed to be inserted from the sea. For this and the Tomahawk-barrage capability, the new SSGN concept is an ideal method for working in the littoral. *U.S. Navy*

The smallest nuclear submarine in the world, *Naval Research Submarine One* (NR-1) arrives in Norfolk to moor next to its mother ship, the *Carolyn Chouest*. The NR-1 is a scientific boat that can work at depths of around 2,600 to 2,700 feet. It carries out scientific and oceanographic missions for the navy and repairs various underwater items of national and naval security. *U.S. Navy*

The former Trident missile firing *Ohio*-class boat in dry-dock at the Puget Sound Navy Shipyard prior to work beginning to convert the boat to an eighteen-thousand-ton SSGN and Special Operations Package. The open missile silos give the public a rare glimpse of where the destruction of the world once was housed in the form of Trident missiles. *Author's collection*

The conventionally powered USS *Bonefish* (SS-582) has just surfaced and is hopelessly ablaze. The date was April 24, 1988, yet the *Bonefish* was no stranger to fires—on June 12, 1982, the boat suffered a major fire in all three engine spaces. The *Bonefish* was one of three diesel-powered teardrop submarines, and the last in the U.S. Navy. *U.S. Navy*

Pearl Harbor on February 1, 1991, and the *Ohio*-class USS *Alabama* (SSBN-731) is moored adjacent to the attack submarine USS *San Francisco* (SSN-711). Behind them at this spacious dock is the *Aegis* missile cruiser USS *Chosin* (CG-45). As many ships that can be safely brought into harbor are there to wish the new commander of the Pacific Fleet well in his assignment. *U.S. Navy*

The *Bonefish* is quickly abandoned as the fire is within the wiring and in the walls. Three men succumbed to the chemically acrid smoke, and the sub ended up a total loss. The sub was towed to port, and a year later decommissioned and then scrapped. A few months later, thirteen more crewmen died of various respiratory ailments. *U.S. Navy*

The USS *Ohio* (SSGN-726) is one of a minimum of four SSGNs that are to be rebuilt from the *Ohio*-class SSBN. The remaining fourteen *Ohio*-class SSBNs will continue to defend the United States from a strategic standpoint. The missiles they have at their command are sufficient to destroy the world twice over!
U.S. Navy

OHIO CLASS
Refitted from a Trident missile SSBN to a guided missile submarine
Operational data: able to fire 154 Tomahawk missiles at tactical targets
Capacity: can carry special operation forces and all of their equipment into littoral or coastal clandestine operations

The decommissioned and deactivated *November*-class attack submarine K-159 had been sitting in the Soviet port of Gremikha for twelve years before being towed to Polarnye for scrapping. Gremikha is an out-of-the-way junkyard of the once-proud Soviet submarine and surface fleets. Destroyers, cruisers, and other craft are run up on the rocks and beaches, and submarines periodically are towed away or sink at their moorings. The K-159 left with a crew of ten on September 18, 2003, and on September 21, the World War II–vintage pontoons broke up in a storm, allowing the sub to founder with nine young conscripts wearing naval uniforms. *Author's collection*

The immense size of the USAF's C-17 is shown with the submarine rescue chamber aboard. Overall, the chamber, technicians, and systems are collectively known as the U.S. Navy Submarine Rescue Chamber Flyaway System. This system can be in most waterways of the world in less than twenty-four hours. *U.S. Navy*

The Royal Danish Navy's HDMS *Saelen* (S-323) is one of three ex-Norwegian *Kobben*-class (type 207) submarines that are small, yet quite lethal. The boat is easily carried on a medium lift ship as it is only 412 tons full load on the surface. It can dive to almost two hundred meters and has the capability of operating in the littoral better than steam-turbine-powered submarines. It has eight bow-mounted torpedo tubes for wire-guided torpedoes. *U.S. Navy*

HDMS *SAELEN*
Commissioned: February 16, 1966, in the Norwegian Navy
Transferred to Denmark in 1986
Propelled by diesel power at 13.5 knots on the surface and 17 knots below the surface
Retrofitted in 2000
Note: The boats of this class have likely been stricken by the time this book goes to press, but they graphically demonstrate the type of undersea craft that will dominate in the shallow coastal waters around the world. The big nuclear-powered submarine has its place, but in the littoral, it is the small conventional powered boat that might tip the balance.

The USS *Frank Cable* (AS-40) moored in Hong Kong harbor. Also on this visit on October 6, 2006, are the USS *Honolulu* (SSN-718) and USS *La Jolla* (SSN-701). The *La Jolla* has the dry-dock shelter attached behind the sail. For the *Honolulu*, this is a bittersweet trip. Its next stop will be its final port of call: Bremerton, and inactivation/scrapping. The *Honolulu* is more than two decades old. *U.S. Navy*

May 2004, and the odd-looking craft known as a weapon-set-to-hit-threat-target (WSTHTT) surfaces after being used for subsurface target practice. Submarine- or surface-ship-launched torpedoes without warheads are fired at this colorful drone stationed under the water and covered with sensors and recording devices. *U.S. Navy*

LITTORAL COMBAT

Littoral Combat

Shortly after 1860, a bloody civil war dominated naval warfare for the fledgling United States; however, its grasp of war at sea was being finely honed. A new type of warship was developed, including the methods for its most effective use: the ironclad monitor and movable turret, and the breech-loading rifled cannon. Much of this innovative naval thought was embodied in the federal warship *Monitor*. This "cheese box on a raft" as it was joked about successfully fought the Confederate ironclad, the CSS *Virginia*. After this action, the jokes stopped. Next it was the victorious use of a submarine by Confederate forces (CSS *H. L. Hunley* versus the USS *Housatonic*).

It would take another three decades until the United States truly ventured out of its front yard to do battle with a major power and the unknown. It was during the war with Spain in 1898 that the U.S. Navy changed its mindset from isolationist-coastal defense to a more international area of operations. There had been skirmishes off North Africa with the Barbary Pirates and exploratory voyages to the Far East, but nothing of the sort where the U.S. Navy would be called to fight abroad with a sizeable force.

The United States and its armed forces were so committed to littoral warfare that ships known as coastal monitors were built to protect American cities from attack by other nations. These vessels, which had less than

Previous page: The USS *Monterey* (M-6), a classic example of a turn-of-the-century coastal monitor. This monster displaced 4,084 tons and was armed with two twelve-inch/.35-caliber guns in a forward firing turret and an aft turret with two ten-inch/.30-caliber guns. In addition, the *Monterey* carried six six-pound quick-firing guns for defense against small-surface threats. The armor plating was quite thick and the ship rode dangerously close to the water. In any seaway, the main deck was flooded, and the trip to the Philippine Islands must have tried the souls of all 218 men aboard. However, this ship was purely to defend the coast of the United States. *U.S. Navy*

Two *Tacoma*-class patrol frigates designed to protect the coastal areas during World War II. The USS *Grand Forks* (PF-11) is the ship nearest the pier at Mare Island and was armed with three three-inch/.50-caliber guns as well as a number of antiair guns and ASW weapons. The *Tacoma* class had a top speed of 20.3 knots and ironically had the same powerplant that the USS *Monterey* had: the vertical triple-expansion engine (the old tried-and-true plant). *U.S. Navy*

A multinational exercise includes two of the warships of the Ghana navy. In the foreground is the ex-USCGC *Woodrush* (WLB-407) commissioned on September 22, 1944, for the U.S. Coast Guard. It was transferred in 2001 and now bears the name *Anzone* (P-30) and is a patrol ship with years of service remaining. In the background is the *Achimota* (P-28) commissioned on March 27, 1981. It was built in Germany, and for its light tonnage (410 tons full load) it is heavily armed with a 76mm/.62-caliber OTO Melara forward and a 40mm/.70-caliber OTO Melara aft. With its three modern diesel engines, it can make thirty knots. Both are serious threats to smugglers and pirates. *U.S. Navy*

Three Vietnamese gunboats are rafted together in the harbor at Na Trang. They are ex-Soviet *Zhuk*-class boats that are forty tons full load, and powered by two diesel engines. The top speed is thirty knots, and they are armed with two twin 12.7mm/.60-caliber MG. *Author's collection*

Kuantan, Malaysia, is a vital petroleum and container port and guarding it are a minimum of two *Spica-M*-class missile patrol boats. The *Ganyang* is moored near the entrance to the naval base. It has been in service since 1974 and is armed with *Exocet* antiship missiles and two guns (57mm and 40mm). Out of sight is the *Rendikar*, which is similarly armed yet with four Exocet missiles. *Author's collection*

two feet of freeboard, had heavy guns as did the major warships of the day. They were designed to defend the nation's cities from marauding fleets with their heavy artillery. In a sense, they were more of a movable battery of field artillery as opposed to being warships; but they were utilized as battleships nonetheless—despite their near-submarine ride in the open sea. (Many did become submarine tenders!)

It would take visionaries and brave souls to move beyond U.S. borders to defend U.S. shores. One such visionary was Theodore Roosevelt. The thought of going forth on the offensive was definitely something out of Roosevelt's diplomatic and naval playbook. Consequently, it was decided that the United States would "free Cuba for the Cubans," from the cruelty of the Old-World colonial power of Spain. It was initially hoped that any battle at sea would be fought locally, but that was not to be the case. Fortunately, Roosevelt, the youthful Assistant Secretary of the Navy, had other ideas, and made arrangements for Admiral George Dewey to rout the

Spanish Navy in the Philippines at the outset of war. This he achieved easily as the Asiatic Navy of Spain was a rotting backwater force that was blown into matchsticks even by Admiral Dewey's extremely poor gunnery (less than 4 percent hits for an entire morning's heavy firing).

Roosevelt and Admiral Dewey did not know exactly how far reaching these moves would take the United States. The country was no longer a nation of isolationists—it was now a real part of the international community and needed a navy to ensure its newfound place in the world. Next would be the voyage of the U.S. Navy's Great White Fleet that took the finest of the U.S. Navy on an around-the-world cruise (ostensibly for peace, but also to showcase American resolve to defend its

shores, people, commerce, and possessions).

Despite the World Wars that would follow in the twentieth century and literally propel the United States into a position of ultimate power due to its phenomenal manufacturing and leadership abilities, the coastal or littoral concept of warfare was never far away. The day of the superpowers that roamed the oceans of the world at will (Great Britain, Spain, France, Germany, the Soviet Union, and NATO; and now at the dawn of the twenty-first century, the United States) has quickly become the spice of history that will occupy several volumes of world history. The day of huge opposing battle lines of progressively larger ships panting to fire tons of munitions at one another is over, and actually was so short lived as to have never existed at all.

The ex-HMS *Plover* (P-240) of the Royal Navy now serves as the Philippine *Apolinario Mabini* (PS-36). This Patrol Craft is involved in search and rescue, antipirate patrols, and antismuggling. These 712-ton full-load craft can make twenty-eight knots and are well armed and suited for their assignments. *U.S. Navy*

FREEDOM CLASS

Crew size: 50 max, including U.S. Navy and Coast Guard personnel

Tops out at less than 4,000 tons (full load)
 Able to operate in water 20 feet deep and at speeds of up to 45 knots

Future ship construction will be as follows:
 All as the monohull or *Freedom* class
 All as the trimaran or *Independence* class
 A combination of both designs
 A split of trimarans and monohulls
 The trimaran is 2,637 tons full load and 419 feet in length.

Note: The *Freedom* series can be armed with a 57mm Bofors gun battery forward, an MH-60 R/S helicopter, unmanned aircraft (e.g., Fire Scout), a Spartan unmanned surface vessel, and a RAM (rolling airframe) twenty-one-missile battery for antiaircraft defense as well as a .50-caliber MG hard points at various locales. The .50-caliber weapons will be for close-in defense against suicide boats and swimmers and to repel boarders. Both LCS designs will be capable of antimine/mine warfare (MIW), antisubmarine (ASW), and antisurface ship (SUW) missions, and take on various modules to enable them to meet these missions.

Marinette, Wisconsin, and the christening of the U.S. Navy's first purpose-built littoral combat ship: the USS *Freedom* (LCS-1). As of April 2007, the *Freedom* class has come under scrutiny for massive cost overruns and equipment that isn't performing according to design. *U.S. Navy*

The *Freedom* was built by the Marinette Marine Shipyard as a semiplaning monohull, yet there is another design by General Dynamics that is a trimaran. The first ship of this design, shown here in this concept art, is the USS *Independence* (LCS-2).

A *Floreal*-class patrol ship in the Royal Moroccan Navy, the *Mohammed V* was built in France at Chantiers de l'Atlantique at St. Nazaire. The ship is 2,950 tons full load with a top speed of twenty knots. Aside from Exocet missiles, the *Mohammed V* is armed with a 76mm/.62-caliber OTO Melara gun battery. *U.S. Navy*

The Peruvian guided-missile corvette *Herrera* (CM-24) moves through the Panama Canal. The 610-ton craft is capable of thirty-seven knots, and is more than sufficiently armed with four Exocet anti-ship missiles, a 76mm/.62-caliber OTO Melara gun battery, and a twin 40mm/.70-caliber OTO Melara Bofors rapid-fire MG. The *Herrera* also has a provision for a four-round MGP-86 SAM antiair missile system. The six ships in this class are very aesthetic in nature. This is generally not the case with today's warships, which often resemble boxes filled with electronics on a scow. *U.S. Navy*

The *Stiletto* (M-80) moves slowly through San Diego Bay toward its base at the Naval Amphibious Center. The *Stiletto* is an experimental littoral combat ship (LCS). It is extremely lightweight due to the use of carbon fiber materials. The vessel was built by M Ship Company, which has a global patent on this technology. It is eighty feet in length with a fifty-foot beam. It can work in extremely shallow waters as it draws a paltry three feet.

The rear of the *Stiletto* opens to allow entry by a powered rubber raft for special operations personnel (SEALs).

STILETTO LITTORAL COMBAT VESSEL
Built under the auspices of the Office of Force Transformation and Special Operations Command (SOCOM)
Top speed: 50 knots on diesel power Based on an "M" hull construction, which channels water under the craft and is superior to a monohull
Note: The M hull reduces drag, shock to the hull and passengers, and a telltale wake. The *Stiletto* is still under examination in San Diego where it will be tested to see if it is capable of deploying underwater unmanned vehicles to hunt mines and also send unmanned aircraft ("manta") aloft to search the immediate area for threats.

One of the two classes of patrol vessels in the new Iraqi Coastal Defense Force. This force has two Assad-class corvettes built in Italy that displace 685 tons full load and are armed with Albatross missiles (SAM), an OTO Melara 76mm/.62-caliber gun battery, Teseo Mark 2 SSM, and a light helicopter. In addition, the force now has five high-speed twenty-seven-meter patrol boats armed with small weapons. Professionals from Great Britain and the USN are teaching the Iraqi Navy the basics of defeating smugglers, pirates, gunrunners, and kidnappers. *U.S. Navy*

U.S. Marines assigned to *RivRon 1* (DSV-2) from Regimental Combat Team 7 patrol the Euphrates River in the Al Anbar Province in Iraq. They use the RHIB 11 meter converted to include an armored center console with two drivers, an aft single or twin .50-caliber MG, a forward semiprotected .50-caliber rapid-fire weapon, and four other hard points for additional machine guns. The training given these marines and seamen is being provided to the Iraqi River Defense Force. *U.S. Navy*

The *Sea Fighter* (FSF-1) is based in San Diego, which has become the home of littoral combat ships and other related craft. At first this rather odd-looking box was dubbed the "X-craft"; however, the Office of Naval Research changed it to *Sea Fighter*—a more appropriate moniker for its capability. *U.S. Navy*

The bridge or pilot house for the *Sea Fighter*. This vessel is not built for creature comfort; however, its ergonomic seating ensures that the crew is none the worse for wear after a day of forty-knot travel. *U.S. Navy*

SEA FIGHTER LITTORAL SURFACE CRAFT
Built by Nichols Brothers Boat Builders, Whidbey Island, Washington
Full-load displacement: 1,400 metric tons
Length: 262 feet
Top speed: 50 knots with 40 knots in Sea State 4
Powered by two gas turbines (surge power) and two diesel engines (cruising power) connected to four waterjet pumps
Armament: two H-60 type helos or unmanned aircraft (VTUAVS), and can be armed with two .50-caliber machine guns (its modules can provide additional firepower)
Crew: 26 max

An inshore patrol craft being built for use in American harbors. A crew of three is provided a high-speed boat with advanced radar and a minimum of three .50-caliber machine guns. *U.S. Navy*

Elements of Task Force 150 (TF-150) based out of Bahrain. This force provides a two thousand–mile coastal patrol along East Africa. Somalia and other nations nearby are almost without any organized government and have let anarchy rule on land and sea. Piracy, theft, murder, and ransom are but a few of the international felonies people in this region perpetrate. *U.S. Navy*

The USNS *Impeccable* (T-AGOS-23) is an ocean-surveillance vessel with swath characteristics. Its primary role is the detection of submarines and other submersible threats through the most sophisticated sonar systems available, including the most powerful towed array developed. The towed array is rumored to have killed several marine mammals due to its sheer resonating power. *U.S. Navy*

USNS *IMPECCABLE*
Built by Friede-Goldman, Halter, Moss Point, Mississippi
Entered service: March 23, 2001
Full-load displacement: 5,380 tons
Top speed: 15 knots
Powerplant: electric power generated by diesel engines
Crew: 22 civilian mariners, 8 contract technicians, and 20 U.S. Navy personnel

The USS *Safeguard* (ARS-50) moored in Hong Kong harbor during July 2006. The *Safeguard* was providing training to local search-and-rescue teams plus shallow- and deep-diving units. The team aboard the *Safeguard* successfully identified the remains of the USS *Lagarto* (SS-371), an American fleet submarine that was sunk by a Japanese escort off the Thailand coast on May 4, 1945. *U.S. Navy*

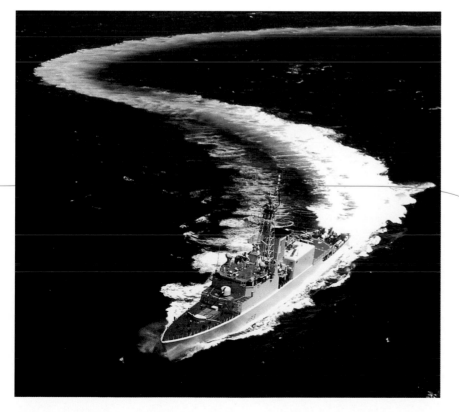

The HMCS *Algonquin* (DDH-283) makes a speedy exit from Pearl Harbor as she joins other ships from eight nations participating in Rim of the Pacific (RIMPAC) 2006 exercises. This exercise has been carried out for years and hones the skills of the navies that participate. This is another example of coalition warfare. *U.S. Navy*

The *Sea Jet* advanced electric ship demonstrator has been tested on a lake in Bayview, Idaho, to observe various hull and engine system combinations. *U.S. Navy*

SEA JET ADVANCED ELECTRIC SHIP DEMONSTRATOR
Under the control of the Office of Naval Research
Length: 133 feet
Note: Rolls-Royce Naval Marine Corporation has provided the underwater discharge pump (AWJ-21). The goal of this system and the hull design is to reduce acoustic (noise signature), improve maneuverability, and increase propulsive efficiency.

The *Sea Slice*, a prototype to the USS *Sea Fighter* and all littoral combat ships (LCSs) under construction and design. Since 1992 private enterprise, including Nichols Brothers of Washington, have been working on the *Sea Slice* concept. Essentially, this vessel is driven by pods on a catamaran hull, which gives it stability and speed (thirty knots in twelve-foot waves). This is vital for any LCS operating in shallow water. The *Sea Slice* has provided crucial data to the LCS builders of the future. *U.S. Navy*

A missile being fired by an improved *Ticonderoga*-class cruiser. The USS *Shiloh* (CG-67) as well as a number of *Arleigh Burke*–class destroyers have or will have this system to defend the United States and its Allies. At present there are two cruisers near Japan plus several improved patriot antimissile batteries available to dull the threat of North Korea's ICBM program.

IMPROVED *TICONDEROGA* CLASS
**Technologically upgraded with the *Aegis*
    ballistic missile defense 3.6-weapon system.**
**System based on "hit to kill"; the new
    systems being installed aboard U.S. cruisers
    and destroyers are part of a layered
    defense against missiles targeting the
    United States and other nations**
Overall hit-to-kill rate: 87.5 percent success

A Standard Missile 3 (SM-3) aboard the USS *Lake Erie* (CG-70). In this test, the *Lake Erie* missile struck the test ICBM at one hundred miles outside of the earth's atmosphere. The ships are not given prior notice of a test launch. In this instance, the ship's crew detected the launch; developed a fire control solution; and, two minutes later, the SM-3 destroyed the ICBM. *U.S. Navy*

The USS *Yorktown* (CG-48) seen in the Pacific in 2002 as the flagship of *UNITAS*. The *Yorktown* proved to be ahead of its time; however, its missile armament was based on the ancient rail launchers. The next twenty-two *Ticonderoga*-class (improved) cruisers were built with the Mark 41 vertical launch system (VLS). *U.S. Navy*

A symbolic gesture that is a strong traditional in the U.S. Navy: the boatswain's mate carries the USS *Yorktown* (CG-48)'s official logbook and ceremonial spyglass off the ship when the ship was decommissioned. The USS *Yorktown* has been a naval unit (cruiser) for twenty years and was one of the earliest ships built around the *Aegis*-supported weapons systems. Since decommissioning on December 3, 2004, the *Yorktown* has moved to the Inactive Ships Site at the Philadelphia Navy Yard. Its fate will be scrapping, use as a target, artificial fish reef, or sale to a foreign power. *U.S. Navy*

THE FUTURE OF NAVAL WARFARE

Again, there is a re-emphasis on coastal warfare that has former "blue water" fighting nations now building ships with moderate armament and virtually no armor. They are designed for inshore combat. After all, more than 80 percent of the world's communication systems, manufacturing operations, population, and commercial centers are within fifty miles of the coastline. The majority of the world's population lives in a littoral environment, and it is that environment that will require protection.

During the apex of blue water combat (World War II to the Cold War), superpowers did not forgo coastal fighting ships. Experimentation continued and new littoral ships were always being designed and built. And today, virtually all of the large surface combatants are museum pieces or have been rendered into washing machines or automobiles. Less than fifty years ago, there were two hundred cruisers in the world's navies. In the twenty-first century there are less than two dozen cruiser-size ships as well as absolutely no battleships at sea. In short, the destroyer or frigate has become the capital ship of today and likely ships of smaller size will take their place as years go by and the price of ship construction continues to skyrocket.

Many nations are making do with smaller ships that have been refitted so many times that the original warship is difficult to find under all of the alterations. A U.S. Navy *Gearing-* or *Sumner*-class destroyer built in the final days of World War II can often be found flying the Taiwanese or other flag, yet every inch of open deck space is crowded with missiles and other weapons.

New materials such as Kevlar (armor); heavy rubber for hulls; fiberglass, and aluminum have come into vogue as replacements for riveted iron or steel or even welded steel.

The day of large American Fleets (e.g., 6th, 7th) roaming unchallenged in the Mediterranean and Western Pacific has ended due to the lack of ships, bases (Subic Bay), and people to operate them. The same holds true with the Russian Navy, which now rusts at its moorings due to a lack of spare parts, no fuel, and ships that have been stripped by their officers and powerful shipyard gangs of easily sold materials (gold, platinum, silver, mercury). To make matters worse, the Vietnamese government expelled the Russian Navy from Da Nang for failure to make rental payments, so their Pacific Fleet has no permanent location in Southeast Asia.

The U.S. Navy has no more than 150 ships capable of sea duty at any one time, and other nations have far fewer. Yet, the problems of piracy, murder, theft, and smuggling remain as they always have. Plus, there are always those nations that decide to flex their muscles at sea which must be dealt with to prevent the cancer of world war. This means coalition forces at sea to meet and beat these difficulties.

The future of the world's navies can be summed up as follows:

No one nation can take complete responsibility for patrolling the entire world's oceans nor should it be allowed to have such dominance.

The United States cannot shoulder the entire burden of being the world's police officer. It is far too expensive for its taxpaying public who is demonstrating growing resentment for funding various operations without even receiving a thank-you note. Alternatively, the more sophisticated nations resent the intrusion of the U.S. military into so many aspects of international diplomacy and politics.

Technology will replace the size and number of weapons in all but the most backward navies.

Warships will require smaller and more technologically savvy crews. The day of the tattooed grizzled chief boatswain's mate holding court with a novice seaman is not over, but will be greatly reduced.

Coalitions of naval forces will be called upon to defeat common enemies (drugs, pirates, escaping brutal dictators). This is where technological advances in communication will serve a common cause.

Information sharing will be a must.

Ships will be required to last up to fifty years and due to modular construction, be able to modernize with ease.

Huge national fleets patrolling the world's oceans will no longer be a luxury. The dream of a thousand-ship navy as put forward recently by the U.S. Navy may be possible; however, it will fly scores of national flags—a potential political minefield.

For decades, navies have done what they could to assist nations during periods of natural disaster. It is clear that conventional resources such as the United Nations (UN), Project HOPE, and Mercy Ships have been overwhelmed. The navies of the world will no doubt include humanitarian assistance in ship design and mission planning for the future. This is a major departure from the classic and traditional roles of the world's navies, but is vital. For the U.S. Navy and all navies in the world that seek to take advantage of new technology and the easy access to it, the turn of the century has been exciting. There are transitional issues to resolve and many challenges to meet and defeat. Navies will do as they always have—meet them head on and at full speed.

BIBLIOGRAPHY

Primary Materials

Private Papers—Manuscripts/Photo Files
Bonner, Carolyn E. Private papers and photos.
Bonner, Kermit H. Private papers and photo collection.

Special Collections—Manuscripts/Photo Collections
Call Bulletin Newspaper File, 1994, Treasure Island
　Museum.
Department of Defense Naval Files.
Pima Air Museum, Tucson, Arizona.
Treasure Island Museum Photo Files, 1994–Various.
U.S. Naval Institute, 1997, 1998, 1999–Various.
U.S. Navy—Office of Information, 1999–Various.
United States of America, National Archives.

Interviews
August, Edward. U.S. Navy Cruiser Sailors
　Association. Various 2006.
Burgress, Rick, Managing Editor, *Sea Power*, Navy
　League. Various 2003–2006.
Commander Surface Force. San Diego and Pearl
　Harbor. August 2005 and March 2006.
Glassy, Pete. Naval Inactive Ships Facility,
　Bremerton, Washington. August 1998.
Pecararo, Joe, Manager, U.S. Maritime Administration
　(MARAD). Suisun Bay Reserve Fleet.
Public Affairs Office. Kitsap Naval Station. August
　2004.
Tauyan, Agnes, Deputy Director, Public Affairs.
Naval Station, Pearl Harbor.

U.S. Government Documents
Dictionary of American Naval Fighting Ships, volume
　V. U.S. Government Printing Office, 1979.
Surface warfare. U.S. Navy, quarterly, 2003–2006.
Submarines. U.S. Navy, monthly, 2005–2006.

Secondary Materials

Books, Monographs, Treaties
Blackman, Paul. *The World's Warships*. Hanover
　House, 1960.
Blackman, Raymond V. B. *Jane's Fighting Ships
　1968–1969*. BPC Publishing, Ltd., 1969.
Bonds, Ray, editor. *Russian Military Power*. Bonanza
　Books, 1982.
Bonner, Kit. *Final Voyages*. Turner Publishing, 1996.

Bonner, Kit, and Carolyn Bonner. *Cold War at Sea*.
　Motorbooks International, 2000.
———. *Great Naval Disasters*. Motorbooks
　International, 1998.
DiCerto, J. J. *Missile Base Beneath the Sea, The Story of
　Polaris*. St. Martins Press, 1967.
Durham, Roger C. *Spy Sub*. Penguin Books, 1996.
English, Adrian. *Armed Forces of Latin America*. Jane's
　Publishing Co. Ltd., 1984.
Erkhammar, Bertil and Ohrelius. *The Royal Swedish
　Navy*. Raben and Sjogren, 1965.
Faulkner, Keith. *Jane's Warship Recognition Guide*.
　Harper Collins Publishing, 1996.
Friedman, Norman. *U.S. Cruisers*. Naval Institute
　Press, 1984.
———. *U.S. Destroyers*. Naval Institute Press, 1982.
———. *U.S. Small Combatants*. Naval Institute Press,
　1987.
Grove, Eric J. *Vanguard to Trident*. Naval Institute
　Press, 1981.
Humble, Richard. *Submarines, The Illustrated History*.
　Basing Hall Books Ltd., 1981.
Jane's Publishing. *Jane's Fighting Ships, 1944–45,
　1947–48, 1955–56, 1979–80, 1968–69,
　1987–88, 1996–97*.
Jordan, John. *Modern U.S. Navy*. Prentice Hall Press,
　1986.
Karnow, Stanley. *Vietnam, A History*. The Viking
　Press, 1983.
Marinha de Guerra Portugesa. *History of the Navy of
　Portugal*. Government of Portugal, 1962.
Mickel, Peter, Hansgeorg Jentschura, and Dieter
　Jung. *Warships of the Imperial Japanese Navy,
　1869–1945*. Naval Institute Press, 1977.
Miller, David. *The Cold War, A Military History*. John
Murray Publishing, 1998.
Moore, John E., Captain R.N. *Jane's American
　Fighting Ships of the Twentieth Century*. Mallard
　Press, 1991.
———. *The Soviet Navy Today*. Stein and Day, 1975.
Morison, Samuel Eliot. *History of the United States
Naval Operations in World War II*, all volumes.
　Atlantic–Little Brown, 1962.
Muir, Malcolm Jr. *Black Shoes and Blue Water*. U.S.
　Government Printing Office, 1996.
Preston, Anthony. *Warships of the World*. Jane's
　Publishing Co. Ltd., 1980.
Schofield, William G., Captain USNR. *Destroyers—*

60 Years. Rand McNally and Company, 1962.
Scott, Harriet, and William F. Scott. *The Armed Forces of the USSR.* Westview Press, 1979.
Sea Power Almanac. Navy League of the United States (NLUS), 1991–2006.
Silverstone, Paul. *U.S. Navy 1945 to the Present.* Arms and Armour Press, 1991.
———. *U.S. Warships Since 1945.* Naval Institute Press, 1987.
Sommervile, Donald. *World War II Day by Day.* Dorset Press, 1989.
Sultzberger, C. L. *The American Heritage Picture History of World War II.* Crown Publishers, 1966.
Sweetman, Jack. *American Naval History.* Naval Institute Press, 1984.
Tazewell, William. *Newport News Shipbuilding, The First Century.* The Mariners Museum, 1986.
Terzibaschitsch, Stephan. *Aircraft Carriers of the U.S. Navy.* Naval Institute Press, 1978.
Utz, Curtis A. *Cordon of Steel.* Naval Historical Center, 1993.
Various Photo-Journalists. *A Day in the Life of the Soviet Union.* Collins Publishers Inc., 1987.
Walker, Martin. *The Cold War.* Owl Books, 1993.
Watts, Anthony. *Axis Submarines.* Arco Publishing Co., 1997.
Wertheim, Eric. *Combat Fleets of the World.* Naval Institute Press, 2005.
Winton, John. *The War at Sea—1939 through 1945.* Pimlico, 1967.
Wright and Logan. *The Royal Navy in Focus 1930–1939, 1940–1949, 1950–1959, 1960–1969.* Maritime Books, 1981.

Articles
Atkinson, James D., and Donovan P. Yeuell, Colonel USA. 1956. Must we have World War III? Naval Institute Proceedings, July.
Author unknown. 1982. Breaking up HM ships, part II. *Warship,* Buxton, IL.
Author unknown. 1997. Russian squadrons in the USA 1863–64. Peace to the Oceans Bulletin, November 12.
Beers, Henry P. 1976. American Naval detachment—Turkey 1919–1924. *Warship International* XIII (3).
Bonner, Kit. 1996. Tonkin Gulf incident. *Sea Classics.* Bureau of Naval Personnel. 1945. *All Hands,* November.
Eller, E. M., Rear Admiral, USN (Ret.). 1955. Soviet bid for the sea. Naval Institute Proceedings, June.
Finney, John W. 1965. Soviets imperil U.S. ships.

Naval Institute Proceedings, June (article reprinted from the *New York Times,* April 4, 1965).
Huan, C., Lt. USN. 1957. The Soviet Union and its submarine force. Naval Institute Proceedings, July.
Matloff, Maurice. 1956. The Soviet Union and the war in the West. Naval Institute Proceedings, March.
Meister, Jurg. 1957. The Soviet Navy in World War II. Naval Institute Proceedings, August.
Navy League of the United States. 1991 and 1997 issues. *Sea Power.*
Parke, Everett A., LTCD, USN. 1960. The unique and vital DER. Naval Institute Proceedings, February.
Sieche, Erwin. 1981. The Type XXI Submarine, part 2. *Warship,* April.
Staff written. 1998. U.S. Naval battle force changes, January–December 1997. Naval Institute Proceedings, May.
Warships International, Fleet Review. Various 2005, 2006. HPC Publishing.
Watt, Donald C. 1964. Stalin's first bid for sea power, 1933–1939. Naval Institute Proceedings, June.
Webber, Mark, Lt. USN. 1965. Kashin class missile frigates. Naval Institute Proceedings, June.
Wheeler, Gerald M. 1957. Naval aviation in the jet age. Naval Institute Proceedings, November.
Winnefeld, James. 1960. The Cold War power spectrum. Naval Institute Proceedings, January.

Web Sites
Russian, Chinese, and U.K. navies Web sites.
U.S. Coast Guard Web site.
U.S. Navy Web site.
U.S. Navy Military—Naval Vessel Register Web sites.

Other
Allison, Graham. 1971. Essence of decision. Grolier Electronic Encyclopedia.
Author unknown. 1993. The Cold War. Grolier Electronic Encyclopedia.
Ely, Abel. 1966. The missile crisis. Grolier Electronic Encyclopedia.
Hamby, Alonzo L. 1993. Cuban missile crisis. Grolier Electronic Encyclopedia.

INDEX OF SHIPS